The
Ad

These stories
– from seventeenth-centu
Pacific island at an unspecified time in the future. In some man is pitting himself against nature; in others, against his own kind; but whatever the background, all the stories are tremendously exciting.

Raymond Wilson is Professor of Education at the University of Reading. As well as writing stories he is a poet, and has compiled a number of poetry anthologies, including *Time's Delights, The Beaver Book of Funny Verse* and *The Beaver Book of Animal Verse*, all published by Beaver.

THE BEAVER BOOK OF ADVENTURE STORIES

compiled by Raymond Wilson

Illustrated by Peter Dennis

Beaver Books

First published in 1982 by
The Hamlyn Publishing Group Limited
London · New York · Sydney · Toronto
Astronaut House, Feltham, Middlesex, England
Reprinted 1983

ISBN 0 600 20479 0

Printed and bound in Great Britain by
Cox & Wyman Ltd, Reading
Set in Times

The original Imperial measurements have been retained in this book. In certain stories they are technical terms which cannot be converted precisely to metric; in the others they have been left for the sake of consistency.

Contents

Acknowledgements

The author and publishers would like to thank the following people for gving permission to include in this anthology material which is their copyright. The publishers have made every effort to trace copyright holders. If we have inadvertently omitted to acknowledge anyone we should be most grateful if this could be brought to our attention for correction at the first opportunity.

Chatto & Windus Limited for 'Gentlemen of the Sealed Knot' from *A Wood by Moonlight* by Geoffrey Trease

Faber and Faber Limited for 'Cry of the Hunters' from *Lord of the Flies* by William Golding

Macmillan Publishers Limited for 'Creature of the Snows' by William Sambrot from *Untravelled Worlds*

Purnell Books for 'Two Useless Pommies' by Kelman Frost from *Boys' Adventure Stories*

Lord Tweedsmuir for 'The Cave of the Rooirand' from *Prester John* by John Buchan

The Executers of the Estate of the late H. G. Wells for 'In the Abyss'

TO BUILD A FIRE

Jack London

Day had broken cold and grey, exceedingly cold and grey, when the man turned aside from the main Yukon trail and climbed the high earth-bank, where a dim and little-travelled trail led eastward through the fat spruce timberland. It was a steep bank, and he paused for breath at the top, excusing the act to himself by looking at his watch. It was nine o'clock. There was no sun nor hint of sun, though there was not a cloud in the sky. It was a clear day, and yet there seemed an intangible pall over the face of things, a subtle gloom that made the day dark, and that was due to the absence of sun. This fact did not worry the man. He was used to the lack of sun. It had been days since he had seen the sun, and he knew that a few more days must pass before that cheerful orb, due south, would just peep above the sky line and dip immediately from view.

The man flung a look back along the way he had come. The Yukon lay a mile wide and hidden under three feet of ice. On top of this ice were as many feet of snow. It was all pure white, rolling in gentle undulations where the ice jams of the freeze-up had formed. North and south, as far as his eye could see, it was unbroken white, save for a dark hairline that curved and twisted from around the spruce-covered island to the south, and that curved and twisted away into the north, where it disappeared behind another spruce-covered island. This dark hairline was the trail – the main trail – that led south five hundred miles to the Chilcoot Pass, Dyea, and salt water; and that led north seventy miles to Dawson, and still on to the north a thousand miles to Nulato, and finally to St Michael, on Bering Sea, a thousand miles and half a thousand more.

But all this – the mysterious, far-reaching hairline trail, the absence of sun from the sky, the tremendous cold, and the strangeness and weirdness of it all – made no impression on the man. It was not because he was long used to it. He was a newcomer in the land, a *chechaquo*, and this was his first winter. The trouble with him was that he was without imagination. He was quick and alert in the things of life, but only in the things, and not in the significances. Fifty degrees below zero meant eighty-odd degrees of frost. Such fact impressed him as being cold and uncomfortable, and that was all. It did not lead him to meditate upon his frailty as a creature of temperature, and upon man's frailty in general, able only to live within certain narrow limits of heat and cold; and from there on it did not lead him to the conjectural field of immortality and man's place in the universe. Fifty degrees below zero stood for a bite of frost that hurt and that must be guarded against by the use of mittens, ear flaps, warm moccasins, and thick socks. Fifty degrees below zero was to him just precisely fifty degrees below zero. That there should be anything more to it than that was a thought that never entered his head.

As he turned to go on, he spat speculatively. There

was a sharp, explosive crackle that startled him. He spat again. And again, in the air, before it could fall to the snow, the spittle crackled. He knew that at fifty below spittle crackled on the snow, but this spittle had crackled in the air. Undoubtedly it was colder than fifty below – how much colder he did not know. But the temperature did not matter. He was bound for the old claim on the left fork of Henderson Creek, where the boys were already. They had come over across the divide from the Indian Creek country, while he had come the round-about way to take a look at the possibilities of getting out logs in the spring from the islands in the Yukon. He would be in to camp by six o'clock; a bit after dark, it was true, but the boys would be there, a fire would be going, and a hot supper would be ready. As for lunch, he pressed his hand against the protruding bundle under his jacket. It was also under his shirt, wrapped up in a handkerchief and lying against the naked skin. It was the only way to keep the biscuits from freezing. He smiled agreeably to himself as he thought of those biscuits, each cut open and sopped in bacon grease, and each enclosing a generous slice of fried bacon.

He plunged in among the big spruce trees. The trail was faint. A foot of snow had fallen since the last sled had passed over, and he was glad he was without a sled, travelling light. In fact, he carried nothing but the lunch wrapped in the handkerchief. He was surprised, however, at the cold. It certainly was cold, he concluded, as he rubbed his numb nose and cheekbones with his mittened hand. He was a warm-whiskered man, but the hair on his face did not protect the high cheekbones and the eager nose that thrust itself aggressively into the frosty air.

At the man's heels trotted a dog, a big native husky, the proper wolf dog, grey-coated and without any visible or temperamental difference from its brother, the wild wolf. The animal was depressed by the tremendous cold. It knew that it was no time for travelling. Its instinct told it a truer tale than was told to the man by the man's judgement. In reality, it was not merely colder than fifty below zero; it was colder than sixty below, than seventy below. It was seventy-five below zero. Since the freezing point is thirty-two above zero, it meant that one hundred and seven degrees of frost obtained. The dog did not know anything about thermometers. Possibly in its brain there was no sharp consciousness of a condition of very cold such as was in the man's brain. But the brute had its instinct. It experienced a vague but menacing apprehension that subdued it and made it slink along at the man's heels, and that made it question eagerly every unwonted movement of the man as if expecting him to go into camp or to seek shelter somewhere and build a fire. The dog had learned fire, and it wanted fire, or else to burrow under the snow and cuddle its warmth away from the air.

The frozen moisture of its breathing had settled on its fur in a fine powder of frost, and especially were its jowls, muzzle, and eyelashes whitened by its crystalled breath. The man's red beard and moustache were likewise frosted, but more solidly, the deposit taking the form of ice and increasing with every warm, moist breath he exhaled. Also, the man was chewing tobacco, and the muzzle of ice held his lips so rigidly that he was unable to clear his chin when he expelled the juice. The result was that a crystal beard of the colour and solidity of amber was increasing its length on his chin. If he fell down it would shatter itself, like glass, into brittle fragments. But he did not mind the appendage. It was the penalty all tobacco chewers paid in that country, and he had been out before in two cold snaps. They had not been so cold as this, he knew, but by the spirit thermometer at Sixty Mile he knew they had been registered at fifty below and at fifty-five.

He held on through the level stretch of woods for several miles, crossed a wide flat of nigger heads, and dropped down a bank to the frozen bed of a small stream. This was Henderson Creek, and he knew he was ten miles from the forks. He looked at his watch. It was ten o'clock. He was making four miles an hour, and he calculated that he would arrive at the forks at half-past twelve. He decided to celebrate that event by eating his lunch there.

The dog dropped in again at his heels, with tail drooping discouragement, as the man swung along the creek bed. The furrow of the old sled trail was plainly visible, but a dozen inches of snow covered the marks of the last runners. In a month no man had come up or down that silent creek. The man held steadily on. He was not much given to thinking, and just then particularly he had nothing to think about save that he would eat lunch at the forks and that at six o'clock he would be in camp with the boys. There was nobody to talk to; and, had there been, speech would have been impossible because of the ice muzzle on his mouth. So he continued monotonously to chew tobacco and to increase the length of his amber beard.

Once in a while the thought reiterated itself that it was very cold and that he had never experienced such cold. As he walked along he rubbed his cheekbones and nose with the back of his mittened hand. He did this automatically, now and again changing hands. But, rub as he would, the instant he stopped his cheekbones went numb, and the following instant the end of his nose went numb. He was sure to frost his cheeks; he knew that, and experienced a pang of regret that he had not devised a nose strap of the sort Bud wore in cold snaps. Such a strap passed across the cheeks, as well, and saved them. But it didn't matter much, after all. What were frosted cheeks? A bit painful, that was all; they were never serious.

Empty as the man's mind was of thoughts, he was keenly observant, and he noticed the changes in the creek, the curves and bends and timber jams, and always he sharply noted where he placed his feet. Once, coming around a bend, he shied abruptly, like a startled horse, curved away from the place where he had been walking, and retreated several paces back along the trail. The creek he knew was frozen clear to the bottom – no creek could contain water in that Arctic winter – but he knew also that there were springs that bubbled out from the hillsides and ran along under the snow and on top of the ice of the creek. He knew that the coldest snaps never froze these springs, and he knew likewise their danger. They were traps. They hid pools of water under the snow that might be three inches deep, or three feet. Sometimes a skin of ice half an inch thick covered them, and in turn was covered by the snow. Sometimes there were alternate layers of water and ice skin, so that when one broke through he kept on breaking through for a while, sometimes wetting himself to the waist.

That was why he had shied in such panic. He had felt the give under his feet and heard the crackle of a snow-hidden ice skin. And to get his feet wet in such a temperature meant trouble and danger. At the very least it meant delay, for he would be forced to stop and build a fire, and under its protection to bare his feet while he dried his socks and moccasins. He stood and studied the creek bed and its banks, and decided that the flow of water came from the right. He reflected awhile, rubbing his nose and cheeks, then skirted to the left, stepping gingerly and testing the footing for each step. Once clear of the danger, he took a fresh chew of tobacco and swung along at his four-mile gait.

In the course of the next two hours he came upon several similar traps. Usually the snow above the hidden pools had a sunken, candied appearance that advertised the danger. Once again, however, he had a close call; and once, suspecting danger, he compelled the dog to go on in front. The dog did not want to go. It hung back until the man shoved it forward, and then it went quickly across the white, unbroken surface. Suddenly it broke through, floundered to one side, and got away to firmer footing. It had wet its forefeet and legs, and almost immediately the water that clung to it turned to ice. It made quick efforts to lick the ice off its legs, then dropped down in the snow and began to bite out the ice that had formed between the toes. This was a matter of instinct. To permit the ice to remain would mean sore feet. It did not know this. It merely obeyed the mysterious prompting that arose from the deep crypts of its being. But the man knew, having achieved a judgement on the subject, and he removed the mitten from his right hand and helped tear out the ice particles. He did not expose his fingers more than a minute, and was astonished at the swift numbness that smote them. It certainly was cold. He pulled on the mitten hastily, and beat the hand savagely across his chest.

At twelve o'clock the day was at its brightest. Yet the sun was too far south on its winter journey to clear the horizon. The bulge of the earth intervened between it and Henderson Creek, where the man walked under a clear sky at noon and cast no shadow. At half-past twelve, to the minute, he arrived at the forks of the creek. He was pleased at the speed he had made. If he kept it up, he would certainly be with the boys by six. He unbuttoned his jacket and shirt and drew forth his lunch. The action consumed no more than a quarter of a minute, yet in that brief moment the numbness laid hold of the exposed fingers. He did not put the mitten on, but, instead, struck the fingers a dozen sharp smashes against his leg. Then he sat down on a snow-covered log to eat. The sting that followed upon the striking of his fingers against his leg ceased so quickly that he was startled. He had had no chance to take a bite of biscuit. He struck the fingers repeatedly and returned them to the mitten, baring the other hand for the purpose of eating. He tried to take a mouthful, but the ice muzzle prevented. He had forgotten to build a fire and thaw out. He chuckled at his foolishness, and as he chuckled he noted the numbness creeping into the exposed fingers. Also, he noted that the stinging which had first come to his toes when he sat down was already passing away. He wondered whether the toes were warm or numb. He moved them inside the moccasins and decided that they were numb.

He pulled the mitten on hurriedly and stood up. He was a bit frightened. He stamped up and down until the stinging returned into the feet. It certainly was cold, was his thought. That man from Sulphur Creek had spoken the truth when telling how cold it sometimes got in the country. And he had laughed at him at the time! That showed one must not be too sure of things. There was no mistake about it, it *was* cold. He strode up and down, stamping his feet and threshing his arms, until reassured by the returning warmth. Then he got out matches and proceeded to make a fire. From the undergrowth, where high water of the previous spring had lodged a supply of seasoned twigs, he got his firewood. Working carefully from a small beginning, he soon had a roaring fire, over which he thawed the ice from his face and in the protection of which he ate his biscuits. For the moment the cold of space was outwitted. The dog took satisfaction in the fire, stretching out close enough for warmth and far enough away to escape being singed.

When the man had finished, he filled his pipe and took his comfortable time over a smoke. Then he pulled on his mittens, settled the ear flaps of his cap firmly about his ears, and took the creek trail up the left fork. The dog was disappointed and yearned back towards the fire. This man did not know cold. Possibly all the generations of his ancestry had been ignorant of cold, of real cold, of cold one hundred and seven degrees below freezing point. But the dog knew; all its ancestry knew, and it had inherited the knowledge. And it knew that it was not good to walk abroad in such fearful cold. It was the time to lie snug in a hole in the snow and wait for a curtain of cloud to be drawn across the face of outer space whence this cold came. On the other hand, there was no keen intimacy between the dog and the man. The one was the toil slave of the other, and the only caresses it had ever received were the caresses of the whip lash and of harsh and menacing throat sounds that threatened the whip lash. So the dog made no effort to communicate its apprehension to the man. It was not concerned in the welfare of the man; it was for its own sake that it yearned back towards the fire. But the man whistled, and spoke to it with the sound of whip lashes, and the dog swung in at the man's heels and followed after.

The man took a chew of tobacco and proceeded to start a new amber beard. Also, his moist breath quickly powdered with white his moustache, eyebrows, and lashes. There did not seem to be so many springs on the left fork of the Henderson, and for half an hour the man saw no signs of any. And then it happened. At a place where there were no signs, where the soft, unbroken snow seemed to advertise solidity beneath, the man broke through. It was not deep. He wet himself halfway to the knees before he floundered out to the firm crust.

He was angry, and cursed his luck aloud. He had hoped to get into camp with the boys at six o'clock, and this would delay him an hour, for he would have to build a fire and dry out his footgear. This was imperative at that low temperature – he knew that much; and he turned aside to the bank, which he climbed. On top, tangled in the underbrush about the trunks of several small spruce trees, was a high-water deposit of dry firewood – sticks and twigs, principally, but also larger portions of seasoned branches and fine, dry, last year's grasses. He threw down several large pieces on top of the snow. This served for a foundation and prevented the young flame from drowning itself in the snow it otherwise would melt. The flame he got by touching a match to a small shred of birch bark that he took from his pocket. This burned even more readily than paper. Placing it on the foundation, he fed the young flame with wisps of dry grass and with the tiniest dry twigs.

He worked slowly and carefully, keenly aware of his danger. Gradually, as the flame grew stronger, he increased the size of the twigs with which he fed it. He squatted in the snow, pulling the twigs out from their entanglement in the brush and feeding directly to the flame. He knew there must be no failure. When it is seventy-five below zero, a man must not fail in his first attempt to build a fire – that is, if his feet are wet. If his feet are dry, and he fails, he can run along the trail for half a mile and restore his circulation. But the circulation of wet and freezing feet cannot be restored by running when it is seventy-five below. No matter how fast he runs, the wet feet will freeze the harder.

All this the man knew. The old-timer on Sulphur Creek had told him about it the previous fall, and now he was appreciating the advice. Already all sensation had gone out of his feet. To build the fire he had been forced to remove his mittens, and the fingers had quickly gone numb. His pace of four miles an hour had kept his heart pumping blood to the surface of his body and to all the extremities. But the instant he stopped, the action of the pump eased down. The cold of space smote the unprotected tip of the planet, and he, being on that unprotected tip, received the full force of the blow. The blood of his body recoiled before it. The blood was alive, like the dog, and like the dog it wanted to hide away and cover itself up from the fearful cold. So long as he walked four miles an hour, he pumped that blood, willy-nilly, to the surface; but now it ebbed away and sank down into the recesses of his body. The extremities were the first to feel its absence. His wet feet froze the faster, and his exposed fingers numbed the faster, though they had not yet begun to freeze. Nose and cheeks were already freezing, while the skin of all his body chilled as it lost its blood.

But he was safe. Toes and nose and cheeks would be only touched by the frost, for the fire was beginning to burn with strength. He was feeding it with twigs the size of his finger. In another minute he would be able to feed it with branches the size of his wrist, and then he could remove his wet footgear, and, while it dried, he could keep his naked feet warm by the fire, rubbing them at first, of course, with snow. The fire was a success. He was safe. He remembered the advice of the old-timer on Sulphur Creek, and smiled. The old-timer had been very serious in laying down the law that no man must travel alone in the Klondike after fifty below. Well, here he was; he had had the accident; he was alone; and he had saved himself. Those old-timers were rather womanish, some of them, he thought. All a man had to do was to keep his head, and he was all right. Any man who was a man could travel alone. But it was surprising, the rapidity with which his cheeks and nose were freezing. And he had not thought his fingers could go lifeless in so short a time. Lifeless they were, for he could scarcely make them move together to grip a twig, and they seemed remote from his body and from him. When he touched a twig, he had to look and see whether or not he had hold of it. The wires were pretty well down between him and his finger ends.

All of which counted for little. There was the fire, snapping and crackling and promising life with every dancing flame. He started to untie his moccasins. They were coated with ice; the thick German socks were like sheaths of iron halfway to the knees; and the moccasin strings were like rods of steel all twisted and knotted as by some conflagration. For a moment he tugged with his numb fingers, then, realising the folly of it, he drew his sheath knife.

But before he could cut the strings, it happened. It was his own fault or, rather, his mistake. He should not have built the fire under the spruce tree. He should have built it in the open. But it had been easier to pull the twigs from the brush and drop them directly on the fire. Now the tree under which he had done this carried a weight of snow on its boughs. No wind had blown for weeks, and each bough was fully freighted. Each time he had pulled a twig he had communicated a slight agitation to the tree – an imperceptible agitation, so far as he was concerned, but an agitation sufficient to bring about the disaster. High up in the tree one bough capsized its load of snow. This fell on the boughs beneath, capsizing them. This process continued, spreading out and involving the whole tree. It grew like an avalanche, and it descended without warning upon the man and the fire, and the fire was blotted out!

Where it had burned was a mantle of fresh and disordered snow.

The man was shocked. It was as though he had just heard his own sentence of death. For a moment he sat and stared at the spot where the fire had been. Then he grew very calm. Perhaps the old-timer on Sulphur Creek was right. If he had only had a trail mate he would have been in no danger now. The trail mate could have built the fire. Well, it was up to him to build the fire over again, and this second time there must be no failure. Even if he succeeded, he would most likely lose some toes. His feet must be badly frozen by now, and there would be some time before the second fire was ready.

Such were his thoughts, but he did not sit and think them. He was busy all the time they were passing through his mind. He made a new foundation for a fire, this time in the open, where no treacherous tree could blot it out. Next he gathered dry grasses and tiny twigs from the high-water flotsam. He could not bring his fingers together to pull them out, but he was able to gather them by the handful. In this way he got many rotten twigs and bits of green moss that were undesirable, but it was the best he could do. He worked methodically, even collecting an armful of the larger branches to be used later when the fire gathered strength. And all the while the dog sat and watched him, a certain yearning wistfulness in its eyes, for it looked upon him as the fire provider, and the fire was slow in coming.

When all was ready, the man reached in his pocket for a second piece of birch bark. He knew the bark was there, and, though he could not feel it with his fingers, he could hear its crisp rustling as he fumbled for it. Try as he would, he could not clutch hold of it. All the time, in his consciousness, was the knowledge that each instant his feet were freezing. This thought tended to put him in a panic, but he fought against it and kept calm. He pulled on his mittens with his teeth, and threshed his arms back and forth, beating his hands with all his might against his sides. He did this sitting down, and he stood up to do it; and all the while the dog sat in the snow, its wolf brush of a tail curled around warmly over its forefeet, its sharp wolf ears pricked forward intently as it watched the man. And the man, as he beat and threshed with his arms and hands, felt a great surge of envy as he regarded the creature that was warm and secure in its natural covering.

After a time he was aware of the first faraway signals of sensation in his beaten fingers. The faint tingling grew stronger till it evolved into a stinging ache that was excruciating, but which the man hailed with satisfaction. He stripped the mitten from his right hand and fetched forth the birch bark. The exposed fingers were quickly going numb again. Next he brought out his bunch of sulphur matches. But the tremendous cold had already driven the life out of his fingers. In his effort to separate one match from the others, the whole bunch fell in the snow. He tried to pick it out of the snow, but failed. The dead fingers could neither touch nor clutch. He was very careful. He drove the thought of his freezing feet, and nose, and cheeks, out of his mind, devoting his whole soul to the matches. He watched, using the sense of vision in place of that of touch, and when he saw his fingers on each side the bunch, he closed them – that is, he willed to close them, for the wires were down, and the fingers did not obey. He pulled the mitten on the right hand, and beat it fiercely against his knee. Then, with both mittened hands, he scooped the bunch of matches, along with much snow, into his lap. Yet he was no better off.

After some manipulation he managed to get the bunch between the heels of his mittened hands. In this fashion he carried it to his mouth. The ice crackled and snapped when by a violent effort he opened his mouth. He drew the lower jaw in, curled the upper lip out of the way, and scraped the bunch with his upper teeth in order to separate a match. He succeeded in getting one, which he dropped on his lap. He was no better off. He could not pick it up. Then he devised a way. He picked it up in his teeth and scratched it on his leg. Twenty times he scratched before he succeeded in lighting it. As it flamed he held it with his teeth to the birch bark. But the burning brimstone went up his nostrils and into his lungs, causing him to cough spasmodically. The match fell into the snow and went out.

The old-timer on Sulphur Creek was right, he thought in the moment of controlled despair that ensued: after fifty below, a man should travel with a partner. He beat his hands, but failed in exciting any sensation. Suddenly he bared both hands, removing the mittens with his teeth. He caught the whole bunch between the heels of his hands. His arm muscles not being frozen enabled him to press the hand heels tightly against the matches. Then he scratched the bunch along his leg. It flared into flame, seventy sulphur matches at once! There was no wind to blow them out. He kept his head to one side to escape the strangling fumes, and held the blazing bunch to the birch bark. As he so held it, he became aware of sensation in his hand. His flesh was burning. He could smell it. Deep down below the surface he could feel it. The sensation developed into pain that grew acute. And still he endured it, holding the flame of the matches clumsily to the bark that would not light readily because his own burning hands were in the way, absorbing most of the flame.

At last, when he could endure no more, he jerked his hands apart. The blazing matches fell sizzling into the snow, but the birch bark was alight. He began laying dry grasses and the tiniest twigs on the flame. He could not pick and choose, for he had to lift the fuel between the heels of his hands. Small pieces of rotten wood and green moss clung to the twigs, and he bit them off as well as he could with his teeth. He cherished the flame carefully and awkwardly. It meant life, and it must not perish. The withdrawal of blood from the surface of his body now made him begin to shiver, and he grew more awkward. A large piece of green moss fell squarely on the little fire. He tried to poke it out with his fingers, but his shivering frame made him poke too far, and he disrupted the nucleus of the little fire, the burning grasses and tiny twigs separating and scattering. He tried to poke them together again, but in spite of the tenseness of the effort, his shivering got away with him, and the twigs were hopelessly scattered. Each twig gushed a puff of smoke and went out. The fire provider had failed. As he looked apathetically about him, his eyes chanced on the dog, sitting across the ruins of the fire from him, in the snow, making restless, hunching movements, slightly lifting one forefoot and then the other, shifting its weight back and forth on them with wistful eagerness.

The sight of the dog put a wild idea into his head. He remembered the tale of the man, caught in a blizzard, who killed a steer and crawled inside the carcass, and so was saved. He would kill the dog and bury his hands in the warm body until the numbness went out of them. Then he could build another fire. He spoke to the dog, calling it to him; but in his voice was a strange note of fear that frightened the animal, who had never known the man to speak in such a way before. Something was the matter, and its suspicious nature sensed danger – it knew not what danger, but somewhere, somehow, in its brain arose an apprehension of the man. It flattened its ears down at the sound of the man's voice, and its restless, hunching movements and the liftings and shiftings of its forefeet became more pronounced; but it would not come to the man. He got on his hands and knees and crawled towards the dog. This unusual posture again excited suspicion, and the animal sidled mincingly away.

The man sat up in the snow for a moment and struggled for calmness. Then he pulled on his mittens, by means of his teeth, and got upon his feet. He glanced down at first in order to assure himself that he was really standing up, for the absence of sensation in his feet left him unrelated to the earth. His erect position in itself started to drive the webs of suspicion from the dog's mind; and when he spoke peremptorily, with the sound of whip lashes in his voice, the dog rendered its customary allegiance and came to him. As it came within reaching distance, the man lost his control. His arms flashed out to the dog, and he experienced genuine surprise when he discovered that his hands could not clutch, that there was neither bend nor feeling in the fingers. He had forgotten for the moment that they were frozen and that they were freezing more and more. All this happened quickly, and before the animal could get away, he encircled its body with his arms. He sat down in the snow, and in this fashion held the dog, while it snarled and whined and struggled.

But it was all he could do, hold its body encircled in his arms and sit there. He realised that he could not kill the dog. There was no way to do it. With his helpless hands he could neither draw nor hold his sheath knife nor throttle the animal. He released it, and it plunged wildly away, with tail between its legs, and still snarling. It halted forty feet away and surveyed him curiously, with ears sharply pricked forward.

The man looked down at his hands in order to locate them, and found them hanging on the ends of his arms. It struck him as curious that one should have to use his eyes in order to find out where his hands were. He began threshing his arms back and forth, beating the mittened hands against his sides. He did this for five minutes, violently, and his heart pumped enough blood up to the surface to put a stop to his shivering. But no sensation was aroused in the hands. He had an impression that they hung like weights on the ends of his arms, but when he tried to run the impression down, he could not find it.

A certain fear of death, dull and oppressive, came to him. This fear quickly became poignant as he realised that it was no longer a mere matter of freezing his fingers and toes, or of losing his hands and feet, but that it was a matter of life and death with the chances against him. This threw him into a panic, and he turned and ran up the creek bed along the old, dim trail. The dog joined in behind and kept up with him. He ran blindly, without intention, in fear such as he had never known in his life.

Slowly, as he ploughed and floundered through the snow, he began to see things again – the banks of the creek, the old timber jams, the leafless aspens, and the sky. The running made him feel better. He did not shiver. Maybe, if he ran on, his feet would thaw out; and, anyway, if he ran far enough, he would reach camp and the boys. Without doubt he would lose some fingers and toes and some of his face; but the boys would take care of him, and save the rest of him when he got there. And at the same time there was another thought in his mind that said he would never get to the camp and the boys; that it was too many miles away, that the freezing had too great a start on him, and that he would soon be stiff and dead. This thought he kept in the background and refused to consider. Sometimes it pushed itself forward and demanded to be heard, but he thrust it back and strove to think of other things.

It struck him as curious that he could run at all on feet so frozen that he could not feel them when they struck the earth and took the weight of his body. He seemed to himself to skim along above the surface, and to have no connection with the earth. Somewhere he had once seen a winged Mercury, and he wondered if Mercury felt as he felt when skimming over the earth.

His theory of running until he reached camp and the boys had one flaw in it: he lacked the endurance. Several times he stumbled, and finally he tottered, crumpled up, and fell. When he tried to rise, he failed. He must sit and rest, he decided, and next time he would merely walk and keep on going. As he sat and regained his breath, he noted that he was feeling quite warm and comfortable. He was not shivering, and it even seemed that a warm glow had come to his chest and trunk. And yet, when he touched his nose or cheeks, there was no sensation. Running would not thaw them out. Nor would it thaw out his hands and feet. Then the thought came to him that the frozen portions of his body must be extending. He tried to keep this thought down, to forget it, to think of something else; he was aware of the panicky feeling that it caused, and he was afraid of the panic. But the thought asserted itself, and persisted, until it produced a vision of his body totally frozen. This was too much, and he made another wild run along the trail. Once he slowed down to a walk, but the thought of the freezing extending itself made him run again.

And all the time the dog ran with him, at his heels. When he fell down a second time, it curled its tail over its forefeet and sat in front of him, facing him, curiously eager and intent. The warmth and security of the animal angered him, and he cursed it till it flattened down its ears appeasingly. This time the shivering came more quickly upon the man. He was losing in his battle with the frost. It was creeping into his body from all sides. The thought of it drove him on, but he ran no more than a hundred feet, when he staggered and pitched headlong. It was his last panic. When he had recovered his breath and control, he sat up and entertained in his mind the conception of meeting death with dignity. However, the conception did not come to him in such terms. His idea of it was that he had been making a fool of himself, running around like a chicken with its head cut off – such was the simile that occurred to him. Well, he was bound to freeze anyway, and he might as well take it decently. With this new-found peace of mind came the first glimmerings of drowsiness. A good idea, he thought, to sleep off to death. It was like taking an anaesthetic. Freezing was not so bad as people thought. There were lots of worse ways to die.

He pictured the boys finding his body next day. Suddenly he found himself with them, coming along the trail and looking for himself. And, still with them, he came around a turn in the trail and found himself lying in the snow. He did not belong with himself any more, for even then he was out of himself, standing with the boys and looking at himself in the snow. It certainly was cold, was his thought. When he got back to the States he could tell the folks what real cold was. He drifted on from this to a vision of the old-timer on Sulphur Creek. He could see him quite clearly, warm and comfortable, and smoking a pipe.

'You were right, old hoss; you were right,' the man mumbled to the old-timer of Sulphur Creek.

Then the man drowsed off into what seemed to him the most comfortable and satisfying sleep he had ever known. The dog sat facing him and waiting. The brief day drew to a close in a long, slow twilight. There were no signs of a fire to be made, and, besides, never in the dog's experience had it known a man to sit like that in the snow and make no fire. As the twilight drew on, its eager yearning for the fire mastered it, and with a great lifting and shifting of forefeet, it whined softly, then flattened its ears down in anticipation of being chidden by the man. But the man remained silent. Later the dog whined loudly. And still later it crept close to the man and caught the scent of death. This made the animal bristle and back away. A little longer it delayed, howling under the stars that leaped and danced and shone brightly in the cold sky. Then it turned and trotted up the trail in the direction of the camp it knew, where were the other food providers and fire providers.

GENTLEMEN OF THE SEALED KNOT

Geoffrey Trease

It all began in that moment when I suddenly became quite certain that I was being watched.

I spun round on my skates and stood there, in the middle of the frozen canal, and looked round warily. The Dutch boys might be up to their tricks again. They often were. You could hardly blame them for taking it out on a solitary English boy when they got the chance. After all, England and Holland had been at war a year or two ago, and they still spoke of our Cromwell as though he were a bogeyman.

I stared round. The canal was lifted high above the frost-grey fields, and I could see a full mile each way across that dull Dutch countryside, until the haze grew too thick to pierce. And in all that landscape nothing stirred: the windmills stood along the dykes, not a sail turning; the willows and poplars might have been wrought iron, for not a branch so much as creaked or quivered in the breathless air.

'Imagination,' I muttered, but I did not believe it. Half-heartedly I tried another figure on my skates. I made rather a mess of it. If the Dutch boys had been watching, crouched down behind the canal-bank, they would have jumped up then, hooting with laughter. They couldn't have resisted it. I could never get them to realise that metal skates were still a complete novelty in England, that most people at home still amused themselves by tying bits of bone to their shoes, and that it wasn't fair to expect the same skill from us on the ice.

No, that last effort of mine would have brought the Bresken lads to their feet, holding their sides and making rude remarks about Engishmen who cut their king's head off but couldn't cut a simple figure on skates.

Yet I still had that eerie sensation that I was being watched. I did another quick jump round, thinking that if it was somebody behind me I would take him by surprise. And this time I caught him – if 'caught' is the word. For he made no attempt to duck down again, but stood there, very tall in a high black hat and a long black cloak, like some giant raven perched on the dyke.

I gasped. I could hardly have been more surprised if the Devil himself had suddenly appeared out of that empty landscape. For a moment we stared at each other. His eyes were dark and brooding, deep set in a swarthy face – yet somehow it was not a sinister face, and there was a kindliness in it. It broke into a smile now, and the man spoke. His voice was quiet, low and musical, even though he spoke in Dutch.

I could only make out something about Englishmen, and answered, haltingly: 'Yes, Mynheer, I am English. I am afraid I cannot speak Dutch very well.'

His eyebrows went up. Then it was my turn to show surprise again, for his next words were in fluent English. He shot out a claw-like hand, beckoning me to the edge of the ice, and peered down into my face. He spoke urgently and, for all his quietness, like one used to command.

'What is your name, boy? What are you doing here? Englishmen seem as common as windmills hereabouts!'

That puzzled me. 'My name's Ralph Selden, sir. I don't know of any other Englishmen here except my father – and he's away at Leyden on business.'

'Selden. . . . Of course, I remember. Your father is William Selden of Cambridge.' He nodded approvingly. 'He came to Holland four months ago to study methods of drainage and dyke-building, so that he may apply them in our own Fens. His mission has the warmest approval of the Lord Protector.'

It was incredible. Father was not famous or anything, yet this stranger had every detail at his fingertips. I began to exclaim. He checked me.

'It is my business to know about Englishmen abroad. Europe is full of wandering Englishmen – traitors who plot with any foreigner to ruin the Commonwealth. Tell me, boy –' he gripped my arm, and his fingers were like steel through his leather glove – 'have you heard of the Sealed Knot?'

'The Sealed Knot?' I shook my head.

He let go my arm. 'It's a conspiracy of the old Cavaliers. They stick at nothing. They tried to murder the Lord Protector as he took his Saturday afternoon ride to Hampton Court. They plotted to seize the port of Hull and let in the Spanish fleet.'

'I know nothing about all that, sir.' The Civil War had finished when I was quite small, and I hadn't realised its fires were still smouldering underground.

'But you are English,' said the man almost fiercely, 'and Cromwell has made England a great country again. Would you want to see her go down once more to rack and ruin?'

'No, sir—'

'Listen. There is something you can do, Ralph Selden.' He pointed to where the lights of the village were beginning to glimmer through the twilight haze.

'Three Englishmen rode into Bresken an hour ago. They have a horse to be re-shod, and they have ordered dinner, so they will be there some time. I would give a great deal to know where they are going, and why. To overhear five minutes of their private talk—'

'Wouldn't that be . . . spying?'

'There are times when honest men must spy – to stop treason and murder, to save innocent lives. . . .' I saw that, and nodded. He smiled down at me and went on in a milder tone. 'Call me a spy if you like, boy. I prefer to call myself an agent of the English Government.' He swept off his hat and bowed solemnly – I had to laugh, it was so funny to see that towering figure bend towards me. 'Permit me to introduce myself, Ralph Selden – Doctor Pharaoh, once of the University of Cambridge, and now of any part of the globe where England has cause to send me! Just now she has sent me to Bresken in Holland, but I think it is the Lord who has sent *you* here to be my helper.'

'Your helper?' I echoed. 'How?'

He chuckled. 'I have one great disadvantage in this work – I am a big man, and, once seen, easily remembered. If I walk into that inn I shall be recognised. Our English gentlemen will keep mum. I shall get nothing for my pains – unless it be a bullet at the first lonely spot on the road when we all move on.'

'They'd do that?'

'They stick at nothing. Only a month or two ago, at Cologne, where the young Prince weaves his plots in exile, they caught one of my friends.'

'What did they do to him?'

'Took him into a wood and shot him.'

I thought for a moment. 'I expect you'd like *me* to go to the inn, and find out anything I can?'

Doctor Pharaoh nodded. 'And report to me at that small tavern at the far end of the village, the Golden Lion. And forget – otherwise – that you have ever seen me or heard my name.'

'I understand, sir.'

And so we parted in the frosty dusk. He was gone like a shadow, and by the time I had unstrapped my skates and stepped over the dyke it was hard to believe that he had ever been there.

The great inn at Bresken was quieter than usual, for the roads were almost as slippery as the ice-bound canals, and nobody was travelling who could avoid it. Even so, there was a good buzz and bustle, for it was a popular meeting-place with the local merchants and farmers, and it was easy for a boy to slip into a quiet corner unnoticed.

If anyone had challenged me, I should have said that I was waiting to deliver a message from my father to one of the millers, when he came in; but in actual fact no one gave me a second glance.

I picked out our three Englishmen at once. Their ringleted hair, their ribbons and laces, their silk-lined boot-tops, all marked them out from that assembly of plainly dressed Dutchmen. Yet, when I studied their faces, bending to meet across the table, I saw that in spite of their fancy clothes and curls there was nothing womanish about them.

I saw the firm jaws and narrowed eyes of men who, as Doctor Pharaoh had said, would stick at nothing. One was portly, red-faced and scar-slashed, a hard-drinking, hard-swearing cavalry officer. Another, the youngest of the three, was lean and pale, with eyes that blazed madly, when he showed excitement, in the light of the candles. But the obvious leader of the group, and the most dangerous, whom the others addressed as Sir James, was a little, oldish, sandy fellow, with the coldest, cruellest face I have ever seen. He made me think of a stoat.

Their dinner was getting near its end. The young man was saying: 'The horses should be ready to move on in another hour.'

'No hurry,' said the red-faced man. 'The wine here is good.'

'That will be your last glass,' Sir James told him firmly. 'Cool heads till the work is done.'

'Cool?' snorted his companion. 'We shall be frozen by the time we reach Tielpoort. We need something to keep the cold out.' But I noticed that his hand fell away from the bottle and he made no further move to refill his glass.

The young man seemed nervous. 'I suppose we are quite certain Wytham will spend tonight in Tielpoort?'

'Where else? He was leaving The Hague this morning. He is in a hurry. That means an early start tomorrow, before dawn. All the better. We shall get him as he steps into his coach. It will be all the easier to slip away if it is still dark.'

'I'm not afraid, Sir James.' But I could see that the young man was as nervous as a cat. He stared round the great room, at the plump Dutchmen warming their breeches and smoking their pipes around the blazing fire, at the maids bustling in and out with drinks and dishes, at the landlord's children playing with a hound in one corner, at myself sitting there with my hat pulled down over my brows, trying to look small and half-asleep. 'I suppose,' I heard him mutter, 'none of these people understand English?'

'If they did,' said the red-faced gentleman irritably, 'what would it matter? Why should they interfere? Anyhow, in a few hours now, it'll be too late for anyone to interfere.' None the less Sir James switched the conversation into French and I could follow it no more.

That should have been a warning to me. For, if it was only Dutchmen they were afraid of, French was no safer than English. But, at the time, I did not stop to think out the full meaning of the move. I knew that I should overhear nothing more, and, Heaven knows, I had heard enough. Someone named Wytham was to be murdered at Tielpoort, first thing in the morning. Wytham? Suddenly the name seemed to click in my brain. Of course – Lord Wytham, the new English Ambassador to Holland! The blood rushed to my cheeks as I realised the full importance of the news.

I had already risen to my feet, trying to act casually, like a boy who was bored and tired of waiting to deliver his message. But now I was so anxious to carry my news to Doctor Pharaoh that I moved more hastily. I collided with one of the serving-girls so that she nearly dropped her tray, and beer went slopping all over my sleeve. I muttered an apology, and she smiled and dabbed my arm with her cloth; then I made my escape just as quickly as I could.

In the doorway I turned and stole a glance at the Englishmen's table. Sir James and the young man were talking hard. But the red-faced fellow had gone.

I stepped out into the cobbled yard. The night air stung my hot cheeks. My mind was racing ahead of my stumbling feet: in imagination, I was already at the far end of the village, reporting to Doctor Pharaoh at the Golden Lion. I was taken completely by surprise when a voice addressed me from the blackness of the archway.

'Just a moment, young fellow.

Instinctively, I paused and turned. And in that moment I was seized in a powerful grip and dragged into the shadows. I smelt hot, wine-laden breath on my face. I knew then, though I could see nothing, that it was the red-faced fellow.

'I thought as much,' he growled. 'You understand English.'

'He *is* English.'

Two figures loomed out of the night, and for an instant I hoped for rescue, and started to cry out, but a leathery hand was clapped over my mouth, and I realised that the newcomers were the other conspirators.

It was Sir James who had spoken. He went on: 'I have just asked that maid. The boy is staying in Bresken. His father is an engineer, studying the dyke-building.' He turned to me. 'Where were you going?'

The rough hand moved to let me answer: 'Home, sir.'

'What other Englishmen are there in this district?'

'None, sir. And my father is away just now.'

There was silence while they considered. Then the young man said anxiously: 'What shall we do with him? He must have heard.'

The red-faced man chuckled brutally. 'Let him study the canals like his Dad. A small hole in the ice, and no questions asked.'

'*No!*' said the young one in a horrified tone. 'We're gentlemen, not murderers! Wytham is bad enough . . . but we do that for the cause.'

'Quiet, both of you,' ordered Sir James. We all stood there in the inky shadow. The hand was over my mouth again, the iron grip never relaxed from the arm twisted behind my back. He thought for a few moments longer. Then he said: 'You must not be so squeamish, Anthony. The servants of the Sealed Knot must do whatever is necessary. But the death of this boy is not necessary – it will only hinder our cause by making fresh enemies. Tie him up, gag him firmly, and shut him up in one of these outhouses. By the time he is found we shall have done our work, and be miles on our road to – where we are going.'

'All right,' growled Red-face sulkily. 'But he'd have made a neat hole in the ice!'

The next few hours were about the worst I have ever spent. How often, playing with other boys, had I been bound and gagged – and how often, after a few squirmings and wrigglings, had I got free from their amateurish knots! This time it was quite different.

I lay helpless in a pitch-black outhouse, half-filled with sawn logs of firewood, mighty hard to lie on. They might at least (I thought to myself bitterly) have stowed me away in the hayloft! I had no idea why the Royalist conspiracy had chosen the name of the Sealed Knot, but in this case it was most fitting. The cords at my wrists and ankles held firm against all my efforts.

The discomfort was bad enough, but I knew it could be only a matter of hours before some inn-servant found me – probably first thing in the morning. It was cold, but for a long time I was hardly aware of that: my useless struggles kept me warm. The worst thing was the knowledge that a man's life depended on me. I knew nothing of Lord Wytham as a person, I cared nothing for the politics of Royalist and Commonwealth men, but I knew that murder was wrong. And if I lay there till a servant found me in the morning, Lord Wytham was a dead man.

Now and again I heard footsteps scrape and slither across the frozen yard, or saw the glint of a lantern through the cracks of the door. I strained at my gag. I could only mumble faintly. Then I managed, by working my legs to and fro, to start a miniature landslide of logs. Part of the heap came rumbling down with a loud noise, and I felt sure that someone would come to investigate, but silence fell again, and nobody came near.

Yet, in the end, it was well they had shut me in the wood-shed and not amid the comfortable hay. There would have been no hatchet in the hayloft. As it was, I suddenly discovered it, and, what was more, the tip of the blade was firmly embedded in the large block on which the servant split the logs!

This was marvellous luck. I could not have done much with a loose hatchet, but this one offered me a blade, fixed quite rigidly, in a position which I could reach with my hands tied behind me. It was not easy. A hatchet used only for splitting firewood is seldom razor-keen, and it cost me a good many minutes of desperate sawing before I felt the tightness at my wrists go suddenly, leaving me with only a few loops of slackened cord.

After that it was easy. Out came the sodden handkerchief from between my teeth, a few seconds were spared to massage the ache from wrists and arms, and another minute freed my ankles. The door of the shed had neither lock nor bolt, only a latch. I burst out into the yard, almost falling full length on the slippery cobbles. The first thing I saw was the full moon coming up over the gabled roof, and I knew then how late it must be. I must have spent hours in that shed. And, as I hurried down the street, I saw that nearly all the lights were out.

The Golden Lion was a small, low-class tavern, and I had never set foot inside it. Nor have I, to this day, for there was no need. A great horse, almost black, stood saddled at the door, and Doctor Pharaoh had his foot in the stirrup.

'The boy!' he muttered under his breath, and put his foot down again. 'I'd given you up. I've just heard – the men slipped away towards Leyden hours and hours ago. I'm after them.'

'They're not going to Leyden,' I panted. 'That's a blind. They're going to Tielpoort.'

'Tielpoort? The opposite direction! Why?'

'The English Ambassador is sleeping there tonight. They mean to assassinate him – early tomorrow morning – as he walks out to his coach.' I stammered out my story as quickly as I could.

He said grimly: 'Civil War is a cruel thing, Ralph Selden. You see where it leads? Englishmen against Englishmen. It did not stop at Naseby, nor at Worcester. It goes on – in the colonies, at the courts of foreign princes, underground, shots in the dark, conspiracies, spying . . . but this is no time to philosophise. Tielpoort, you said? A long way.'

Only then did I start calculating, setting the distance against the time. 'You can't do it,' I groaned.

'I must do it.'

'Not with the roads in this state. They're like glass.'

He swung his vast bulk into the saddle. 'Sir James and his friends will do it.'

'But they've had hours of start. They could walk their horses. *You* can't.'

'I must trust in the Lord,' he said simply. 'Goodbye, Ralph Selden, you've done a good night's work.'

He touched the mare, and she started forward, and down the moonlit street they clattered at a speed which made me wince. I walked after them, simply because it was the way to the farm where we were lodged, and I wanted to find my skates where Red-face had kicked them when he seized me under the archway. They were still there all right, and I walked on out of Bresken, suddenly conscious of how cold and hungry and tired I was. My adventure had ended as abruptly as it had started.

But it proved otherwise.

As I passed from the village street into the open country and saw the long, moonlit road striped with the shadows of the poplars, I was aware of another dark shadow just in front, a patch which moved as I drew nearer. I heard a low groan from the ditch, and hesitated, scared lest some new danger lurked there. I felt I had had enough for one night. Then I saw that the moving shadow was Doctor Pharaoh's black mare, and, as I hurried forward again, the man himself stumbled to his feet. He recognised me at once.

'You were right, boy,' he said between his teeth, and I knew he was in pain, 'the road is like glass. Hold her a moment, will you? I think my arm is broken.' And to my amazement I saw he was trying to climb into the saddle again.

'You can't ride like that, sir!'

'I must.' But his right arm hung useless, and he was a great, heavy man. I had no strength to help him up.

The moon was riding high in an almost cloudless heaven. The silvered landscape lay under it, bright as day. I knew it must be very late now. It was a roundabout route to Tielpoort – the road bent this way and that, avoiding marshes and unbridged canals. I knew it was no use my offering to ride in his place. No horseman could now reach Tielpoort before dawn. I said so, as he paused in his struggle to mount, and leant panting and sweating against the mare's flank.

'Then the Ambassador is done for!' he groaned. 'Think, boy, is there no other way?'

Then in a twinkling, the idea came. 'Yes, sir! I've just

thought – the canal! It runs to Tielpoort, straight as a die! Half the distance of the road—'

'I can't ride along a canal—'

'It's frozen—'

'And more slippery than the road!'

'I don't mean to ride,' I said impatiently. 'I mean *skate.*'

As I said that, I knew for certain that it must be I who went to Tielpoort. There could be few Englishmen in the world with enough experience of skating to cover all those miles. I was not sure I could do it myself. But I could try.

Doctor Pharaoh wasted no time in argument. He asked one or two sensible questions, and then the matter was settled. To my relief, he had provisions in his saddle-bag, and, as I listened to his instruction, I was able to eat, and sip the spirit-and-water he carried in his flask. 'Take it,' he said, 'and the food – but only a sip, mind, when you feel chilled.' We said goodbye then, rather solemnly, he mumbling some text from the Bible, and I ran down across the fields, my feet scrunching the frozen furrows, to where the canal lay between its high banks, a narrow white stripe running to the far horizon.

I knelt, strapped on my skates, and started, wondering very much if I should ever reach the end of my journey, and what that end would be.

The Dutch, of course, travelled long distances on their skates. I had never gone farther than a mile or two from home, though I suppose, in a long afternoon's skating, I must have covered a good distance up and down. But I had never done anything like this before.

It was an eerie journey. The whole world was asleep except myself. Not a light glimmered from the villages. The stark poplars stood up like skeletons, the windmills spread their motionless arms like crucifixes. And on and on, unbending as a moonbeam, the great canal stretched from horizon to horizon. If I had been the man in the moon, I could not have felt more lonely.

On, on . . . mile after mile . . . under bridges, over the desolate salt-marshes, once through a sleeping town with high, curved gables and paved quays, and a church spire catching the light like a dagger . . . on, on, with aching legs and thumping heart – just a minute's pause to sit quivering on the dyke, to tear ravenously at bread and meat, to sip the fiery drink in the Doctor's flask . . . then on again, on, on. . . .

The moon was sinking. Longer and longer were the crossed shadows of the windmills. My pace slackened. There was a great ache in my ankles, my thighs, in every part of my weary body. Then I remembered those three faces plotting murder over the candlelit table at the inn, and I forced myself forward again.

Forward! The moon was nearly down. Only its upper rim gleamed yellow above the horizon. Then even that was gone, and icy darkness flooded the landscape, and I knew I had barely an hour to dawn.

At least there was no fear of missing my way. Smaller drains and ditches forked left and right, but the main canal ran ever forward, and even without the moon it was possible to see that ghostly grey causeway stretching ever onwards. Was that a light, pricking the gloom like a golden star, perhaps a mile in front? Yes! And there was another. A third over there to the left. . . .

The world was waking up again. I was approaching a town. Heaven be praised, it must be Tielpoort, no other!

Ten minutes later I was unfastening my skates on the broad, tree-lined quay of the deserted fish-market.

It was not hard to find the principal inn where the English Ambassador had slept. Its galleried courtyard was already astir. Lanterns bobbed everywhere. Even as I dragged my weary legs under the archway, the ostlers were harnessing four powerful Flemish beasts to a heavy coach.

I plucked a servant by the sleeve and asked for the Ambassador, only to be brushed aside with an impatient laugh. Then I tackled a lanky, cross-looking fellow, a secretary to judge from the papers in his hand.

'Are you crazy?' he said roughly. Then with surprise: 'Why, you're English!'

'I must see the Ambassador,' I whispered. 'At once.'

He gave me a narrow look, summing me up. Then, without further dispute he led me by way of a staircase to a handsome upper room, where a small white-haired gentleman was eating hurriedly as he stood, already cloaked and hatted for the road.

I bowed as I had been taught to do to a nobleman. 'My lord, I have a message – from Doctor Pharaoh.'

The old gentleman started. 'Pharaoh? That faithful watch-dog. Close the door, Mr Benson, and stand against it. Well, boy?'

My knees felt suddenly like water. I clutched at a chair-back. 'Three men are waiting to shoot you as you go out to your coach, my lord. They are agents of the Sealed Knot. Sir James Borrowdale and two others.'

The secretary exclaimed. Lord Wytham nodded as if he was not entirely surprised. Then he said in a calm tone: 'My pistols, Mr Benson.'

'Surely, my lord, you will not risk yourself—'

'Mr Benson,' said the old gentleman with dignity, 'here in Holland I represent England. England does not slip out by back ways, nor does she cower indoors.'

'But wait, while I have these men arrested, my lord—'

'Who will arrest them? We are not at home. And on what charge can they be arrested before they have fired a shot? Warn the escort, Mr Benson, but do not give the alarm. Leave the rest to me.'

The last scene of the drama I watched from the safety of the inn-gallery, peering down into the courtyard. The coach was drawn up near the foot of the outside staircase. Early as the hour was, the courtyard was full of townspeople curious to see Cromwell's Ambassador. The escort, four armed men, kept a space clear from the stairs to the coach-step. I scanned the faces of the crowd eagerly. At once I picked up Red-face, then the blazing eyes of the pale young man, then, a pace or two away, Sir James. . . .

Everyone was turned towards the main staircase, as first the Ambassador's boxes were carried down and then Mr Benson descended, with a backward glance as though expecting to see his master just behind. Yet, when the Ambassador appeared, no one saw him but myself.

He had come down another way, entered his coach from the opposite side, and now stood framed in its open doorway. A pistol glinted in each hand. He spoke quietly, and every head spun round in amazement.

'Well, Sir James, have you something to say to me?'

Their pistols snapped almost together. I heard Sir James's bullet shatter the window of the coach. The next moment the whole courtyard was in an uproar, as escort and conspirators battled to reach one another through the panic-stricken, neutral crowd.

They got away, the three gentlemen of the Sealed Knot. I fancy that Lord Wytham preferred them to escape, once they had shown their hand. They had horses ready outside, and galloped away over the fields into the dawn. Only Red-face's horse stumbled, and I had the great satisfaction of seeing him thrown head-first into a duck-pond – and it was no small hole in the ice *he* made. He came out, cursing and dripping, remounted and fled after the others before his pursuers could catch up with him.

I was wiping the tears of laughter from my eyes when I heard the quiet voice of the Ambassador at my side:

'I think, my boy, England owes you a good breakfast – and perhaps a little more.'

THE CAVE OF THE ROOIRAND

John Buchan

David Crawfurd, when a boy in Scotland, sees one night a black preacher performing magic rites by a fire on a deserted beach. He escapes from the preacher, who pursues him with a knife. Years later, on the ship taking him to his first job, in South Africa, David again sees the black minister, the Reverend John Laputa, whose mysterious movements are focused on the area around Blaauwildebeestefontein, a lonely outpost where David is a storekeeper. David is constantly spied on, and learns from Captain Arcoll, a British Intelligence officer who disguises himself as an old Kaffir, that a rising is planned, to re-establish the empire of Prester John, King of Abyssinia in the fifteenth century. The leader of the rising is Laputa. David ingeniously discovers Laputa's plans, sends a message to Captain Arcoll, and cheats his way into the Cave of Rooirand, where there is a great gathering.

This extract has been chosen for its vividness and excitement, but it was published early in the century (1909) and some of its vocabulary reflects the superior attitude adopted by white men towards Africans at that time. Certainly, such vocabulary is insensitive by today's standards. Even so, we should note that Buchan not only presents Prester John as a toweringly majestic figure, but puts into the priest's mouth a ringing condemnation of 'white infamy', which has debased and enslaved his heroic race by imposing 'unjust laws' and wrongfully seizing land from its 'rightful possessors'.

I was roused by a sudden movement. The whole assembly stood up, and each man clapped his right hand to his brow and then raised it high. A low murmur of 'Inkulu' rose above the din of the water. Laputa strode down the hall, with Henriques limping behind him. They certainly did not suspect my presence in the cave, nor did Laputa show any ruffling of his calm. Only Henriques looked weary and cross. I guessed he had had to ride my pony.

The old man whom I took to be the priest advanced towards Laputa with his hands raised over his head. A pace before they met he halted, and Laputa went on his knees before him. He placed his hands on his head, and spoke some words which I could not understand. It reminded me, so queer are the tricks of memory, of an old Sabbath-school book I used to have which had a picture of Samuel ordaining Saul as king of Israel. I think I had forgotten my own peril and was enthralled by the majesty of the place – the wavering torches, the dropping wall of green water, above all, the figures of Laputa and the Keeper of the Snake, who seemed to have stepped out of an antique world.

Laputa stripped off his leopard skin till he stood stark,

a noble form of a man. Then the priest sprinkled some herbs on the fire, and a thin smoke rose to the roof. The smell was that I had smelled on the Kirkcaple shore, sweet, sharp, and strange enough to chill the marrow. And round the fire went the priest in widening and contracting circles, just as on that Sabbath evening in spring.

Once more we were sitting on the ground, all except Laputa and the Keeper. Henriques was squatting in the front row, a tiny creature among so many burly savages. Laputa stood with bent head in the centre.

Then a song began, a wild incantation in which all joined. The old priest would speak some words, and the reply came in barbaric music. The words meant nothing to me; they must have been in some tongue long since dead. But the music told its own tale. It spoke of old kings and great battles, of splendid palaces and strong battlements, of queens white as ivory, of death and life, love and hate, joy and sorrow. It spoke, too, of desperate things, mysteries of horror long shut to the world. No Kaffir ever forged that ritual. It must have come straight from Prester John or Sheba's queen, or whoever ruled in Africa when time was young.

I was horribly impressed. Devouring curiosity and a lurking nameless fear filled my mind. My old dread had gone. I was not afraid now of Kaffir guns, but of the black magic of which Laputa had the key.

The incantation died away, but still herbs were flung on the fire, till the smoke rose in a great cloud, through which the priest loomed misty and huge. Out of the smoke-wreaths his voice came high and strange. It was as if some treble stop had been opened in a great organ, as against the bass drone of the cataract.

He was asking Laputa questions, to which came answers in that rich voice which on board the liner had preached the gospel of Christ. The tongue I did not know, and I doubt if my neighbours were in better case. It must have been some old sacred language – Phoenician, Sabaean, I know not what – which had survived in the rite of the Snake.

Then came silence while the fire died down and the smoke eddied away in wreaths towards the river. The priest's lips moved as if in prayer: of Laputa I saw only the back, and his head was bowed.

Suddenly a rapt cry broke from the Keeper. 'God has spoken,' he cried. 'The path is clear. The Snake returns to the House of its Birth.'

An attendant led forward a black goat, which bleated feebly. With a huge antique knife the old man slit its throat, catching the blood in a stone ewer. Some was flung on the fire, which had burned small and low.

'Even so,' cried the priest, 'will the king quench in blood the hearth-fires of his foes.'

Then on Laputa's forehead and bare breast he drew a bloody cross.

'I seal thee,' said the voice, 'priest and king of God's people.'

The ewer was carried round the assembly, and each dipped his finger in it and marked his forehead. I got a dab to add to the other marks on my face.

'Priest and king of God's people,' said the voice again, 'I call thee to the inheritance of John. Priest and king was he, king of kings, lord of hosts, master of the earth. When he ascended on high he left to his son the sacred Snake, the ark of his valour, to be God's dower and pledge to the people whom He has chosen.'

I could not make out what followed. It seemed to be a long roll of the kings who had borne the Snake. None of them I knew, but at the end I thought I caught the name of Tchaka the Terrible, and I remembered Arcoll's tale.

The Keeper held in his arms a box of curiously wrought ivory, about two feet long and one broad. He was standing beyond the ashes, from which, in spite of the blood, thin streams of smoke still ascended. He opened it, and drew out something which swung from his hand like a cascade of red fire.

'Behold the Snake,' cried the Keeper, and every man in the assembly, excepting Laputa and including me, bowed his head to the ground and cried 'Ow.'

'Ye who have seen the Snake,' came the voice, 'on you is the vow of silence and peace. No blood shall ye shed of man or beast, no flesh shall ye eat till the vow is taken from you. From the hour of midnight till sunrise on the second day ye are bound to God. Whoever shall break the vow, on him shall the curse fall. His blood shall dry in his veins, and his flesh shrink on his bones. He shall be an outlaw and accursed, and there shall follow him through life and death the Avengers of the Snake. Choose ye, my people; upon you is the vow.'

By this time we were all flat on our faces, and a great cry of assent went up. I lifted my head as much as I dared to see what would happen next.

The priest raised the necklace till it shone above his head like a halo of blood. I have never seen such a jewel, and I think there has never been another such on earth. Later I was to have the handling of it, and could examine it closely, though now I had only a glimpse. There were fifty-five rubies in it, the largest as big as a pigeon's egg, and the least not smaller than my thumbnail. In shape they were oval, cut on both sides *en cabochon*, and on each certain characters were engraved. No doubt this detracted from their value as gems, yet the characters might have been removed and the stones cut in facets, and these rubies would still have been the noblest in the world. I was no jewel merchant to guess their value, but I knew enough to see that here was wealth beyond human computation. At each end of the string was a great pearl and a golden clasp. The sight absorbed me to the exclusion of all fear. I, David Crawfurd, nineteen years of age, and assistant-storekeeper in a back-veld dorp, was privileged to see a sight to which no Portuguese adventurer had ever attained. There, floating on the smoke-wreaths, was the jewel which may once have burned in Sheba's hair.

As the priest held the collar aloft, the assembly rocked with a strange passion. Foreheads were rubbed in the dust, and then adoring eyes would be raised, while a kind of sobbing shook the worshippers. In that moment I learned something of the secret of Africa, of Prester John's empire and Tchaka's victories.

'In the name of God,' came the voice, 'I deliver to the heir of John the Snake of John.'

Laputa took the necklet and twined it in two loops round his neck till the clasp hung down over his breast. The position changed. The priest knelt before him, and received his hands on his head. Then I knew that, to the confusion of all talk about equality, God has ordained some men to be kings and others to serve. Laputa stood naked as when he was born. The rubies were dulled against the background of his skin, but they still shone with a dusky fire. Above the blood-red collar his face had the passive pride of a Roman emperor. Only his great eyes gloomed and burned as he looked on his followers.

'Heir of John,' he said, 'I stand before you as priest and king. My kingship is for the morrow. Now I am the priest to make intercession for my people.'

He prayed – prayed as I never heard man pray before – and to the God of Israel! It was no heathen fetish he was invoking, but the God of whom he had often preached in Christian kirks. I recognised texts from Isaiah and the Psalms and the Gospels, and very especially from the two last chapters of Revelation. He pleaded with God to forget the sins of his people, to recall the bondage of Zion. It was amazing to hear these bloodthirsty savages consecrated by their leader to the meek service of Christ. An enthusiast may deceive himself, and I did not question his sincerity. I knew his heart, black with all the lusts of paganism. I knew that his purpose was to deluge the land with blood. But I knew also that in his eyes his mission was divine, and that he felt behind him all the armies of Heaven.

'*Thou hast been a strength to the poor,*' said the voice, '*a refuge from the storm, a shadow from the heat, when the blast of the Terrible Ones is as a storm against a wall.*

'Thou shalt bring down the noise of strangers, as the heat in a dry place; . . . the branch of the Terrible Ones shall be brought low.

'And in this mountain shall the Lord of Hosts make unto all people a feast of fat things, a feast of wines on the lees, of fat things full of marrow.

'And He will destroy in this mountain the face of the covering cast over all people, and the veil that is brought over all nations.

'And the rebuke of His people shall He take away from off all the earth; for the Lord hath spoken it.'

I listened spellbound as he prayed. I heard the phrases familiar to me in my schooldays at Kirkcaple. He had some of the tones of my father's voice, and when I shut my eyes I could have believed myself a child again. So much he had got from his apprenticeship to the ministry. I wondered vaguely what the good folks who had listened to him in churches and halls at home would think of him now. But there was in the prayer more than the supplications of the quondam preacher. There was a tone of arrogant pride, the pride of the man to whom the Almighty is only another and greater Lord of Hosts. He prayed less as a suppliant than as an ally. A strange emotion tingled in my blood, half awe, half sympathy. As I have said, I understood that there are men born to kingship.

He ceased with a benediction. Then he put on his leopard-skin cloak and kilt, and received from the kneeling chief a spear and shield. Now he was more king than priest, more barbarian than Christian. It was as a king that he now spoke.

I had heard him on board the liner, and had thought his voice the most wonderful I had ever met with. But now in that great resonant hall the magic of it was doubled. He played upon the souls of his hearers as on a musical instrument. At will he struck the chords of pride, fury, hate, and mad joy. Now they would be hushed in breathless quiet, and now the place would echo with savage assent. I remember noticing that the face of my neighbour, 'Mwanga, was running with tears.

He spoke of the great days of Prester John, and a hundred names I had never heard of. He pictured the heroic age of his nation, when every man was a warrior and hunter, and rich kraals stood in the spots now desecrated by the white man, and cattle wandered on a thousand hills. Then he told tales of white infamy, lands snatched from their rightful possessors, unjust laws which forced the Ethiopian to the bondage of a despised caste, the finger of scorn everywhere, and the mocking word. If it be the part of an orator to rouse the passion of his hearers, Laputa was the greatest on earth. 'What have ye gained from the white man?' he cried. 'A bastard civilisation which has sapped your manhood; a false religion which would rivet on you the chains of the slave. Ye, the old masters of the land, are now the servants of the oppressor. And yet the oppressors are few, and the fear of you is in their hearts. They feast in their great cities, but they see the writing on the wall, and their eyes are anxiously turning lest the enemy be at their gates.' I cannot hope in my prosaic words to reproduce that amazing discourse. Phrases which the hearers had heard at mission schools now suddenly appeared, not as the white man's learning, but as God's message to His own. Laputa fitted the key to the cipher, and the meaning was clear. He concluded, I remember, with a picture of the overthrow of the alien, and the golden age which would dawn for the oppressed. Another Ethiopian empire would arise, so majestic that the white man everywhere would dread its name, so righteous that all men under it would live in ease and peace.

My mind was mesmerised by this amazing man. I could not refrain from shouting with the rest. Indeed I was a convert, if there can be conversion when the emotions are dominant and there is no assent from the brain. I had a mad desire to be of Laputa's party. Or rather, I longed for a leader who should master me and make my soul his own, as this man mastered his followers.

As the voice ceased there was a deep silence. The hearers were in a sort of trance, their eyes fixed glassily on Laputa's face. It was the quiet of tense nerves and imagination at white-heat. I had to struggle with a spell which gripped me equally with the wildest savage. I forced myself to look round at the strained faces, the wall of the cascade, the line of torches. It was the sight of Henriques that broke the charm. Here was one who had no part in the emotion. I caught his eye fixed on the rubies, and in it I read only a devouring greed. It flashed through my mind that Laputa had a foe in his own camp, and the Prester's collar a votary whose passion was not that of worship.

The next thing I remember was a movement among the first ranks. The chiefs were swearing fealty. Laputa took off the collar and called God to witness that it should never again encircle his neck till he had led his people to victory. Then one by one the great chiefs and indunas advanced, and swore allegiance with their foreheads on the ivory box. Such a collection of races has never been seen. There were tall Zulus and Swazis with *ringkops* and feather head-dresses. There were men from the north with heavy brass collars and anklets; men with quills in their ears, and earrings and nose-rings; shaven heads, and heads with wonderfully twisted hair; bodies naked or all but naked, and bodies adorned with skins and necklets. Some were light in colour, and some were black as coal; some had squat Negro features, and some thin, high-boned Arab faces. But in all there was the air of mad enthusiasm. For a day they were forsworn from blood, but their wild eyes and twitching hands told their future purpose.

For an hour or two I had been living in a dream-world. Suddenly my absorption was shattered, for I saw that my time to swear was coming. I sat in the extreme back row at the end nearest the entrance, and therefore I should naturally be the last to go forward. The crisis was near when I should be discovered, for there was no question of my shirking the oath.

Then for the first time since I entered the cave I realised the frightful danger in which I stood. My mind had been strung so high by the ritual that I had forgotten all else. Now came the rebound, and with shaky nerves I had to face discovery and certain punishment. In that moment I suffered the worst terror of my life. There was much to come later, but by that time my senses were dulled. Now they had been sharpened by what I had seen and heard, my nerves were already quivering and my fancy on fire. I felt every limb shaking as 'Mwanga went forward. The cave swam before my eyes, heads were multiplied giddily, and I was only dimly conscious when he rose to return.

Nothing would have made me advance, had I not feared Laputa less than my neighbours. They might rend me to pieces, but to him the oath was inviolable. I staggered crazily to my feet, and shambled forwards. My eye was fixed on the ivory box, and it seemed to dance before me and retreat.

Suddenly I heard a voice – the voice of Henriques – cry, 'By God, a spy!' I felt my throat caught, but I was beyond resisting.

It was released, and I was pinned by the arms. I must have stood vacantly, with a foolish smile, while unchained fury raged round me. I seemed to hear Laputa's voice saying, 'It is the storekeeper.' His face was all that I could see, and it was unperturbed. There was a mocking ghost of a smile about his lips.

Myriad hands seemed to grip me and crush my breath, but above the clamour I heard a fierce word of command.

After that I fainted.

TWO USELESS POMMIES

Kelman Frost

'Hey, you two useless pommies, ride on as fast as you can to the tank, and tell whoever's in charge that we'll be in with around two thousand head just before sundown! Tell him to see there's plenty of water, or I'll want to know the reason why.'

The harsh voice of Prickly Jack rasped the ears, and his scowl was no more pleasant, but the two young Englishmen to whom he shouted showed no resentment. The elder raised his hand in acknowledgement, and they both kicked their heels to their horses. One did not argue with an Australian herd-boss.

'Useless pommies, he called us!' grunted Dick Grant. 'Did you hear that?'

Ivor looked round and grinned at his brother, and his backward glance took in the wide expanse of barren, sun-scorched country across which the herd was being driven.

'Don't take any notice of what Prickly Jack says. His bark's worse than his bite. All Englishmen out here are called pommies, and we'd have been sent back a long time ago if we'd been useless.'

Dick tried to bring his bay mare alongside the other's big grey. Ivor was three years older than he, and long in the leg, but it was obvious that the grey was too strong for him. Whenever they moved faster than a walk, Ivor found it difficult to prevent his mount running away with him. Even in the midday heat of the outback, the grey was still full of spirit.

'Why's he called Prickly Jack?' asked Dick, when their mad gallop had subsided to a canter.

Ivor laughed.

'He's named after those five-cornered burrs which smother us whenever we go into the bush. They're like his temper, five-cornered, and all with points, but he's not so bad really. They say he's the best herd-boss in the Territory.'

There was a proprietary note in Ivor's voice. He had been in Australia two years now, and liked to show his newly-arrived younger brother that he was beginning to understand the country. He was proud that he worked on the Peake Downs Station, one of the biggest cattle ranges in the Northern Territory.

This was Dick's first cattle drive. Every year a herd of beef cattle was driven from Peake Downs to Dajarra, in Queensland, for trucking. They travelled great distances, and the drive usually took three months, during which time the stockmen lived rough and adventurously. They had to cross one of the most barren regions in the continent, to meet all extremes of climate, and most importantly to get a high percentage of their cattle to Dajarra in good condition.

It was a challenge that tested to the utmost the stockmen and their aborigine assistants. This experience was something that Dick had not dared hope for when he had joined Ivor a few months earlier, but here they were somewhere on the Barkly Tableland, more than halfway on their journey.

The countryside was barren in the extreme, with little but spinifex in the way of vegetation. Rarely indeed did the cattle get a good feed, and there had been losses, but not more than expected. Before they were finally shipped east the beasts would be rested and fattened.

Water was the main problem. Cattle could live on short rations for a considerable time, but they could not live without water. For that reason water-points had been established a day's march apart, and it was towards one of these, known as G17, that they headed.

The first thing they saw of it was the windmill which drew up the water from a deep artesian well. These were a familiar sight along the route, as were the tanks, reservoirs which were kept filled by the pumps. These were usually artificial, although in places natural hollows had been strengthened with concrete and used for water storage.

Towards the end of a day, when the cattle could smell the water, the whole herd would plunge forward at redoubled speed.

Presently the tank itself was visible, and they were glad to see that there was plenty of water glittering in the sunlight. Not for the first time, Dick marvelled that the wardens of these tanks could stand the intense loneliness of their lives. There was only one man at each water-point, whose duty it was to see that the tank was kept filled and the windmill in running order. These men lived entirely alone for months at a time, seeing nobody but the stockmen as the herds passed through. Yet there were always applicants for the job, and some of them were very strange characters.

As the boys drew nearer they saw two small, stone-built huts at the foot of the windmill, but there was no sign of life.

'The warden must be asleep,' grunted Ivor, trying to

check the headlong rush of his horse, excited by the proximity of water. 'They usually come out before this.'

The horses' hoofs thundered on the hard ground. Some brumbies – wild horses – broke from the scrub on the far side of the tank, and Ivor's big grey gave a shrill, angry neigh, fighting hard to get his head in order to go after them.

However, thirst helped Ivor to master him, and they pulled up beside some stunted gum-trees. As they dismounted and led their horses to the water, they looked towards the huts. There was no movement in the one that was used as living quarters.

'Coo-oooo-eeee!' called Dick, proud of his vocal accomplishment.

The door remained closed. Nothing stirred.

They did not allow the horses to drink too much, and tugged them away from the tank. The water looked very tempting, and they would have liked nothing better than to strip off their clothes and plunge in. But first they had a mission. Their horses were tied to a rail, and they went forward to the hut. Any fear they may have had that it was unoccupied was dispelled when someone inside cleared his throat.

Ivor knocked in perfunctory fashion, and lifted the latch.

'Hullo, there!' he called.

The man lying on the bunk lowered the book he was reading and looked over the top. He was pale-faced and hollow-cheeked; the horn-rimmed spectacles he was wearing went strangely with his surroundings. His sparse hair hung low over his high forehead, and he scowled irritably.

'What d'you want?'

Dick saw his brother stiffen. This was not the sort of welcome that they usually received from these lonely guardians of the waterholes, who were always pleased to see visitors.

There were books everywhere, most of them paper-covered. There must have been several hundred in the small cabin.

'The Peake Downs outfit is coming up fast behind us,' said Ivor. 'We've got about two thousand head, but I see there's plenty of water in the tank. They'll be here before sundown.'

The man put down his book and swung his feet from the bunk. When he stood up they were surprised by his height. He was well over six feet, and very lanky, a fact which was exaggerated by the dirty pyjamas which were his sole garment.

'The water's not for cattle!' he growled, and reached behind a curtain which was stretched across a corner of the hut. 'It belongs to the brumbies and the 'roos.'

'Eh – what?' asked Ivor, uncertain that he had heard rightly. 'What did you . . . ?'

He broke off and backed into Dick, for the man had snatched a rifle from behind the curtain, and he immediately swung it to cover them. For the first time they noticed how his blue eyes blazed behind the thick lenses of his glasses.

'You heard what I said!' He held the rifle at waist level, with his finger on the trigger. It was a .303 Lee Enfield, a surplus British Army weapon, a type which was used extensively in the outback for shooting kangaroos. 'Do you think I'm going to let two thousand cattle mop up that water when the brumbies and the 'roos go thirsty, not to mention the birds? Get going!'

Speechless, they found themselves outside the cabin. It dawned on them that they were dealing with a crazy man. They had heard of loneliness driving men out of their senses, but it had never occurred to them that they would encounter one of these unfortunate persons.

'Listen here—!' began Ivor.

'Shut up!' The man's tone was ugly, and he nodded towards the other hut, which was used for storage. 'Get inside there! You can't fool Jim Devlin with soft talk. I know my rights. That water belongs to me, and I decide who drinks it. If I say no cattle, I mean no cattle! If I see as much as a pair of horns over the ridge, I'll put a bullet between 'em. The same goes for any stockmen.'

Dick, who was partially screened by his brother, made a sudden dive to one side, hoping to get round the back of the hut and divide the man's attention. With incredible swiftness the rifle jerked, there was a crack, and he felt his wide-brimmed hat knocked from his head.

The bolt rattled and the spent cartridge flew from the breech. Blue eyes blazed as Devlin barked:

'Get back beside your cobber, or you're a dead 'un! I can't miss at this range. Inside the hut – both of you!'

'Come on, Dick!' muttered Ivor, and took him by the arm. 'Better do as he says.'

The door opened to their touch, and they went inside. A few crates, and an empty keg, were the only things on the floor. A saddle hung on one of the walls. The door slammed behind them, and they heard Devlin fitting padlock and chain through heavy staples. Muttering, he strode away.

The only light came through a small square opening in one of the walls. Ivor looked at Dick, and his expression was one of deep concern.

'What do you know about this?' he exploded. 'He's as crazy as a loon! We've got to warn the others before they ride into trouble.'

They looked at the walls, but they were solid and impregnable. The door was massive, and they had seen that the chain was equally strong. Dick stood on tiptoe and peered through the opening. He was able to see past the tank to the ridge over which the herd would soon be approaching.

Jim Devlin was walking towards the gum-trees, rifle in hand. On arrival he began to flatten some of the mulga scrub, every now and then pausing to stare at the ridge.

'He's going to post himself where he can shoot anything that comes over the ridge,' muttered Ivor, looking over Dick's shoulder. 'He means business. We've got to get out of here and disarm him before it's too late.'

Their eyes wandered to the roof, which was of

corrugated iron bolted to a stout wooden frame firmly attached to the walls. It was necessary to fasten securely the roof of any building exposed to the sudden gales which sometimes sprang up in these parts, otherwise it would be ripped off in a matter of minutes.

'It's our only chance,' grunted Dick. 'Let me get up and see what I can do.'

He upended the keg and stood upon it, which enabled him to press with both hands against the underside of the roof. He heaved with all his might, using the strength of his legs as well as his arms, but the corrugated iron did not budge.

Breathing hard, red in the face, he desisted from his efforts, and examined the roof fastenings closely.

'The holes round the bolts have rusted at the edges,' he reported. 'If we could push hard enough we ought to be able to break through.'

'Wait!' Ivor was piling one crate upon another. 'Get down and stand the keg on top of these. We've both got to raise ourselves high enough to get our backs under the roof. If we can shove together, something ought to give.'

When they had piled the boxes and the keg high enough for their purpose, they climbed up side by side. There was enough room for them to stand in a bent position with their backs against the underside of the same strip of corrugated iron. They braced themselves with their hands on the wall.

'Now . . .' muttered Ivor. 'Heave . . .!'

They strained upwards, wondering if the crates would collapse under them. The corrugated iron creaked and complained, but there was very little movement in it.

'Harder . . .!' gasped Dick, and they made a mighty effort.

Something tore away with a metallic screech. One of the bolts had pulled through the iron sheeting, which bent upwards, letting in a shaft of sunlight.

'He'll hear that!' panted Dick, and would have jumped down, but his brother checked him and raised a corner of the roofing.

He was able to get his head through the opening, and looked towards the tank. Jim Devlin was still hidden among the scrub. Evidently the sound had not carried to him, or he was too busy watching the ridge to take notice.

'It's all right. . . .' muttered Ivor, then tensed as he saw something moving on the skyline. 'Glory, they're coming!'

A horseman had arrived on the ridge, and even at that distance they could recognise him as Prickly Jack. For a moment he stood out clearly against the cloudless sky, then from the edge of the tank there came the crack of a rifle. Prickly Jack's horse reared, spun about, and disappeared as another shot rang out.

'We've got to stop him before he does further damage!' hissed Ivor, levering at the bent edge of the roofing. 'We've got to make this hole bigger.'

Frenziedly they heaved, and their united efforts tore another bolt through the rusting metal. The opening was large enough for their purpose. Ivor climbed out first, with Dick not far behind.

Prickly Jack and his horse had disappeared. Whether either had been hit it was impossible to tell, but they guessed that Devlin would have his rifle aligned on the same spot, with his finger on the trigger.

Once outside, they dropped to the ground and started towards the tank at a crouching run. There was no cover until they reached the bulrushes which fringed the expanse of water on that side. Into these they plunged, and lay panting.

Silently they watched, and presently saw the mulga scrub move just ahead, close to the edge of the tank. Ivor's hand clamped down on Dick's arm. The head of Jim Devlin came up. He was paler than ever, and his eyes were unnaturally bright, but they were keen behind his glasses as he looked towards the hut. The barrel of his rifle showed above the bushes. He held it ready for instant use.

Fortunately the slope of the roof of the hut hid the

upturned edge of the corrugated iron, and the man noticed nothing unusual. He turned towards the ridge, and ducked down again.

'He's waiting for 'em,' whispered Dick. 'How can we get to him without being seen? There's no cover.'

His brother was scowling at the water beside them.

'Break me off a long, hollow reed,' he ordered, 'and don't make a noise about it.'

As he reached for a suitable reed, Dick was surprised to see Ivor taking off his boots and shirt. His eyes widened, and when Ivor blew through the reed that he handed him, he could not restrain his curiosity.

'What are you going to do?'

'The only cover is the water. If I can crawl along the foot of the bank, keeping under the water, I can get close enough to jump him. Be ready to rush forward and help me as soon as I shout. Between us we ought to be able to manage him.'

'But—' began the younger boy.

'No time to waste! Prickly Jack will be sending his men round by the flank, and if they try to rush Devlin there'll be shooting and killing. Our way there will be no bloodshed.'

He slid backwards into the water, making no splash, holding one end of the reed in his mouth and letting the other end remain above the surface. He could then breathe while keeping out of sight.

Dick watched the tip of the projecting reed moving slowly along the foot of the bank. It made scarcely a ripple, not enough to draw the attention of the man who was watching the distant ridge.

Unless Jim Devlin stood up and looked down directly into the water, he would not see Ivor.

Now the reed was approaching the point where the crazed guardian of the tank was hiding. Dick licked his lips, and rose on his hands and knees to be in readiness.

Away to the left, beyond the strip of mulga scrub, there was a hoarse shout. One of the stockmen had worked round to that side. His shout had been to attract

Devlin's attention while the others came in from the right. Prickly Jack had no idea who was holding him up, and he was not going to wait to find out. He wanted action, and he would not hesitate to shoot whoever had fired at him. Poor Jim Devlin was likely to be shot down like a mad dog unless the boys could save him.

The shout could not have been heard by one underwater, but he chose that moment to make his dramatic appearance. Water poured from him as he rushed the bank, but it did not lessen his speed. Before Devlin had time to realise what was happening, the sodden dripping figure had leapt on him and grasped the rifle with both wet hands.

Dick hurled himself forward the moment his brother emerged. He arrived as they were wrestling for the Lee Enfield, and jumped unhesitatingly on the man's back, locking his arms about the scrawny neck.

Devlin gave a strangled cry, let go his hold on the rifle, and fell backwards. Ivor tossed the rifle behind him and leapt on top of the prostrate Aussie, who was threshing about like a maddened bull.

There was a thud of hoofs as the stockmen rode in.

'What goes on here?' came the rasping voice of Prickly Jack, as he dropped from the saddle. 'What do you pommies think you're doin'?'

Ivor saw his opportunity, swung a clenched fist to Devlin's exposed jaw and had the satisfaction of seeing him go limp. He turned to the herd-boss with a faint grin. Prickly Jack looked fighting mad.

'Devlin's gone crazy,' Ivor told him. 'He shot at you. He's got the idea that all this water belongs to him. We didn't want any bloodshed, so. . . .'

Rapidly he explained what had happened, while the circle of bronzed faces showed more and more astonishment as the stockmen listened.

'Well, I'll be durned . . . !' grunted Prickly Jack, when Ivor had finished. 'Not bad goin' for a couple o' pommies!'

'Useless pommies!' put in Dick.

The herd-boss scowled.

'I'm not sayin' you mightn't learn to be of use,' he admitted. 'You probably saved someone from bein' shot today, anyway. . . . Tucker, Smithy, pick Devlin up an' get the poor blighter in out of the sun! I can never understand why more of these tank wardens don't go crackers! . . . You others bring in the cattle!'

Within ten minutes two thousand thirst-crazed cattle were milling round the tank, bellowing and snorting as they sucked in the life-giving water. In the hut Jim Devlin was recovering consciousness, and blinking about him in puzzled fashion, no longer violent.

Ivor's hefty punch to the jaw had shaken up his addled wits, and he was almost normal again.

'Don't tell him what he did,' Prickly Jack told them round the fire that night. 'He thinks he had a touch of the sun. Best let him go on thinkin' that. We'll take him down to Dajarra with us. He's due for a long rest before he comes back here – if he ever does.'

On the other side of the fire the two brothers exchanged glances. They were discovering that under his prickly exterior the herd-boss had a kindly heart. Furthermore, they knew that they had earned a high place in his estimation.

THE SIEGE OF THE ROUND-HOUSE

Robert Louis Stevenson

David Balfour, who tells the story, is orphaned and leaves his Scottish village to seek his fortune. First he makes his way to the House of Shaws, near Edinburgh, where his miserly Uncle Ebenezer, far from helping him, deliberately endangers his life and then has him kidnapped by the captain of a brig. The brig runs down a boat in the fog and only one man survives – a Jacobite called Alan Breck, who is as quick and nimble with his cutlass as he is with his tongue. The lives of both Alan Breck, who carries gold in his belt, and David Balfour, are threatened by the villainous captain and his crew, who prepare to attack them in the round-house*.

But now our time of truce was come to an end. Those on deck had waited for my coming till they grew impatient;

* A cabin on the quarterdeck.

and scarce had Alan spoken, when the captain showed face in the open door.

'Stand!' cried Alan, and pointed his sword at him.

The captain stood, indeed; but he neither winced nor drew back a foot.

'A naked sword?' says he. 'This is a strange return for hospitality.'

'Do ye see me?' said Alan. 'I am come of kings; I bear a king's name. My badge is the oak. Do ye see my sword? It has slashed the heads off mair Whigamores than you have toes upon your feet. Call up your vermin to your back, sir, and fall on! The sooner the clash begins, the sooner ye'll taste this steel throughout your vitals.'

The captain said nothing to Alan, but he looked over at me with an ugly look. 'David,' said he, 'I'll mind this;' and the sound of his voice went through me with a jar.

Next moment he was gone.

'And now,' said Alan, 'let your hand keep your head, for the grip is coming.'

Alan drew a dirk, which he held in his left hand in case they should run in under his sword. I, on my part, clambered up into the berth with an armful of pistols and something of a heavy heart, and set open the window where I was to watch. It was a small part of the deck that I could overlook, but enough for our purpose. The sea had gone down, and the wind was steady and kept the sails quiet; so that there was a great stillness in the ship, in which I made sure I heard the sound of muttering voices. A little after, and there came a clash of steel upon the deck, by which I knew they were dealing out the cutlasses and one had been let fall; and after that, silence again.

I do not know if I was what you call afraid; but my heart beat like a bird's, both quick and little; and there was a dimness came before my eyes which I continually rubbed away, and which continually returned. As for hope, I had none; but only a darkness of despair and a sort of anger against all the world that made me long to sell my life as dear as I was able. I tried to pray, I remember, but that same hurry of my mind, like a man running, would not suffer me to think upon the words; and my chief wish was to have the thing begin and be done with it.

It came all of a sudden when it did, with a rush of feet and a roar, and then a shout from Alan, and a sound of blows and someone crying out as if hurt. I looked back over my shoulder, and saw Mr Shuan in the doorway crossing blades with Alan.

'That's him that killed the boy!' I cried.

'Look to your window!' said Alan; and as I turned back to my place, I saw him pass his sword through the mate's body.

It was none too soon for me to look to my own part; for my head was scarce back at the window, before five men, carrying a spare yard for a battering-ram, ran past me and took post to drive the door in. I had never fired with a pistol in my life, and not often with a gun; far less against a fellow-creature. But it was now or never; and just as they swang the yard, I cried out, 'Take that!' and shot into their midst.

I must have hit one of them, for he sang out and gave back a step, and the rest stopped as if a little disconcerted. Before they had time to recover, I sent another ball over their heads; and at my third shot (which went as wide as the second) the whole party threw down the yard and ran for it.

Then I looked round again into the deck-house. The whole place was full of the smoke of my own firing, just as my ears seemed to be burst with the noise of the shots. But there was Alan, standing as before; only now his sword was running blood to the hilt, and himself so swelled with triumph and fallen into so fine an attitude, that he looked to be invincible. Right before him on the floor was Mr Shuan, on his hands and knees; the blood was pouring from his mouth, and he was sinking slowly lower, with a terrible, white face; and just as I looked, some of those from behind caught hold of him by the heels and dragged him bodily out of the round-house. I believe he died as they were doing it.

'There's one of your Whigs for ye!' cried Alan; and then turning to me, he asked if I had done much execution.

I told him I had winged one, and thought it was the captain.

'And I've settled two,' says he. 'No, there's not enough blood let; they'll be back again. To your watch, David. This was but a dram before meat.'

I settled back to my place, recharging the three pistols I had fired, and keeping watch with both eye and ear.

Our enemies were disputing not far off upon the deck, and that so loudly that I could hear a word or two above the washing of the seas.

'It was Shuan bauchled* it,' I heard one say.

And another answered him with a 'Wheesht, man! He's paid the piper.'

After that the voices fell again into the same muttering as before. Only now, one person spoke most of the time, as though laying down a plan, and first one and then another answered him briefly, like men taking orders. By this, I made sure they were coming on again, and told Alan.

'It's what we have to pray for,' said he. 'Unless we can give them a good distaste of us, and done with it, there'll be nae sleep for either you or me. But this time, mind, they'll be in earnest.'

By this, my pistols were ready, and there was nothing to do but listen and wait. While the brush lasted, I had not the time to think if I was frighted; but now, when all was still again, my mind ran upon nothing else. The thought of the sharp swords and the cold steel was strong in me; and presently, when I began to hear stealthy steps and a brushing of men's clothes against the round-house wall, and knew they were taking their places in the dark, I could have found it in my mind to cry out aloud.

All this was upon Alan's side; and I had begun to think my share of the fight was at an end, when I heard some-one drop softly on the roof above me.

* Bungled.

Then there came a single call on the sea-pipe, and that was the signal. A knot of them made one rush of it, cutlass in hand, against the door; and at the same moment, the glass of the skylight was dashed in a thousand pieces, and a man leaped through and landed on the floor. Before he got his feet, I had clapped a pistol to his back, and might have shot him, too; only at the touch of him (and him alive) my whole flesh misgave me, and I could no more pull the trigger than I could have flown.

He had dropped his cutlass as he jumped, and when he felt the pistol, whipped straight round and laid hold of me, roaring out an oath; and at that either my courage came again, or I grew so much afraid as came to the same thing; for I gave a shriek and shot him in the midst of the body. He gave the most horrible, ugly groan and fell to the floor. The foot of a second fellow, whose legs were dangling through the skylight, struck me at the same time upon the head; and at that I snatched another pistol and shot this one through the thigh, so that he slipped through and tumbled in a lump on his companion's body. There was no talk of missing, any more than there was time to aim; I clapped the muzzle to the very place and fired.

I might have stood and stared at them for long, but I heard Alan shout as if for help, and that brought me to my senses.

He had kept the door so long; but one of the seamen, while he was engaged with others, had run in under his guard and caught him about the body. Alan was dirking him with his left hand, but the fellow clung like a leech. Another had broken in and had his cutlass raised. The door was thronged with their faces. I thought we were lost, and catching up my cutlass, fell on them in flank.

But I had not time to be of help. The wrestler dropped at last; and Alan, leaping back to get his distance, ran upon the others like a bull, roaring as he went. They broke before him like water, turning, and running, and falling one against another in their haste. The sword in his hands flashed like quicksilver into the huddle of our fleeing enemies; and at every flash there came the scream of a man hurt. I was still thinking we were lost, when lo! they were all gone, and Alan was driving them along the deck as a sheepdog chases sheep.

Yet he was no sooner out than he was back again, being as cautious as he was brave; and meanwhile the seamen continued running and crying out as if he was still behind them; and we heard them tumble one upon another into the forecastle, and clap-to the hatch upon the top.

The round-house was like a shambles; three were dead inside, another lay in his death agony across the threshold; and there were Alan and I victorious and unhurt.

He came up to me with open arms. 'Come to my arms!' he cried, and embraced and kissed me hard upon both cheeks. 'David,' said he, 'I love you like a brother. And O, man,' he cried in a kind of ecstasy, 'am I no a bonny fighter?'

Thereupon he turned to the four enemies, passed his sword clean through each of them, and tumbled them out of doors one after the other. As he did so, he kept humming and singing and whistling to himself, like a man trying to recall an air; only what *he* was trying was to make one. All the while, the flush was in his face, and his eyes were as bright as a five-year-old child's with a new toy. And presently he sat down upon the table, sword in hand; the air that he was making all the time began to run a little clearer, and then clearer still; and then out he burst with a great voice into a Gaelic song.

. . . I knew no word of the Gaelic; but what with the long suspense of the waiting, and the scurry and strain of our two spirits of fighting, and more than all, the horror I had of some of my own share in it, the thing was no sooner over than I was glad to stagger to a seat. There was that tightness on my chest that I could hardly breathe; the thought of the two men I had shot sat upon me like a nightmare; and all upon a sudden, and before I had a guess of what was coming, I began to sob and cry like any child.

Alan clapped my shoulder, and said I was a brave lad and wanted nothing but a sleep.

'I'll take the first watch,' said he. 'Ye've done well by me, David, first and last. . . .'

So I made up my bed on the floor; and he took the first spell, pistol in hand and sword on knee, three hours by the captain's watch upon the wall. Then he roused me up, and I took my turn of three hours; before the end of which it was broad day, and a very quiet morning, with a smooth, rolling sea that tossed the ship and made the blood run to and fro on the round-house floor, and a heavy rain that drummed upon the roof. All my watch there was nothing stirring; and by the banging of the helm, I knew they had even no one at the tiller. Indeed (as I learned afterwards) there were so many of them hurt or dead, and the rest in so ill a temper, that Mr Riach and the captain had to take turn and turn like Alan and me, or the brig might have gone ashore and nobody the wiser. It was a mercy the night had fallen so still, for the wind had gone down as soon as the rain began. Even as it was, I judged by the wailing of a great number of gulls that went crying and fishing round the ship, that she must have drifted pretty near the coast or one of the islands of the Hebrides; and at last, looking out of the door of the round-house, I saw the great stone hills of Skye on the right hand, and, a little more astern, the strange isle of Rum.

HOSTAGE WITH A PLAN

Raymond Wilson

Jean Grey was a weekly boarder at Simonside Comprehensive, a small school, as Comprehensives go, in a Scottish Border town where, according to the English teacher, there had been grim happenings centuries ago – looting, burning, hanging, as reivers from north and south fought over cattle in the Coquet valley. So much violence seemed to have exhausted the town for ever, it was so still and brooding now, crouched among the mute hills all around. There wasn't even much traffic to speak of, except for the couple of school buses waiting at the gates to take her schoolfriends and her to remote villages, still deader than the town. Not to mention, buried deep in the Cheviot valleys, the farmsteads and sheilings lying at the end of rough tracks, suitable only for a Land Rover or cart.

It was Friday. As the day scholars were dropped at the nearer crossroads and hamlets, they waved and shouted to the boarders, whose homes were more distant, that they'd see them on Monday. There were only five left on the bus when it finally crawled into Alwinton, a stone-built village dreaming in the autumn afternoon as the sun sloped low on the rim of hills. With its hundred or so inhabitants, it was the nearest centre of civilisation for Jean and her family, whose farm lay eight miles farther up the valley. Once a year Alwinton came to life for the sheepdog trials, but now, Jean reflected, they'd only recently finished and there'd be no more excitement till the winter snows walled the whole family in their farmstead, with no possibility of school for her and plenty to do helping her father dig sheep out of the drifts. Last year the snows had persisted for more than a month. A helicopter had dropped fodder and medicines for the animals. *That* had been exciting! But she'd had to make the most of it for months afterwards. For nothing ever happened, she grumbled to herself; not even at school. And despite the old ballads and stories they read in English lessons, nothing would persuade her that the solemn stillness of the hills where she lived had ever been shattered by violence and deadly feuds.

The twins – Mary and Maggie Tully – went off across the fields as they did each Friday. Their cottage was by the sheepdip, less than a mile away. Meanwhile, Johnny Pringle swarmed into the back of the Land Rover after his friend Bill Rutherford, whose father always gave him a lift. Mr Rutherford called across: 'Your father's late, Jeannie. Shall I drive ye out that way?'

She hated putting people to trouble. 'No thank you, Mr Rutherford. We arranged on the phone last night that Dad'll meet me, so I'd better wait.'

'Something urgent on the farm, I daresay. Must be, since he's always in good time for ye. Ye're certain ye want to wait, Jeannie?'

Jean nodded. Mr Rutherford hesitated, then gave her a broad smile before driving off. From the rear, Johnny

Pringle waved exaggeratedly, like the clown he was. He jabbed Bill Rutherford to do the same, but Bill didn't wave or so much as look in her direction. She was old enough to guess why, and young enough to find it funny.

Twenty minutes passed. Mrs Hetherington, the innkeeper's wife, came to the door a second time to exclaim at how long her father was taking. 'Come along in and we'll try phoning. Who knows but he's had a breakdown on the way. And not surprising, either, what with all those ruts, worse than a ploughed field beneath his tyres.'

But the phone didn't ring at the farmhouse. There was only the unremitting whine you got when the wires were brought down by snow.

Mrs Hetherington pressed her to have a cup of tea, but Jean felt embarrassed and wouldn't. 'I'll walk up the road to the track and meet him,' she explained, hitching her satchel on her shoulder and stepping back outside.

The evening was turning the colour of slate. 'Ye'd do a sight better to wait, lassie,' Mrs Hetherington protested; but Jean was already moving off, independent, smiling her apologies.

Believing that her father would appear at any moment, she walked steadily, without haste. After two miles the tarmac ended. The darkness massed and moved through the valley in a tide several shades blacker than the sky above the hills. She continued to walk, keeping on the outside edge of the track for fear of spraining an ankle in its pitted surface. Remembering an old legend about the ghost of a shepherd hanged, so they said, in a five-hundred-year-old oak, not half a mile from where she passed, she began to sense inside herself rather more excitement than she'd bargained for; and though she told herself she wasn't frightened, her pace quickened, keeping time with her heartbeats.

If her father had been coming for her, she'd have heard the engine disturbing the silence of the hills, and she'd have seen headlights lancing the darkness miles away. Even if the Land Rover had broken down on the way, her father could easily have walked ahead to meet her. Unless he'd brought her two young brothers with him, George, aged five, and Alec, only three; in which case, he might have taken them back home, knowing she was old enough to find her own way there. She was thirteen, after all; too old to fear the dark.

But she had to admit to feeling strangely disquieted. The fact was, she didn't quite believe the explanations she was making to herself. Moreover, she hadn't even found an explanation of why the telephone wasn't working. The sombreness of the hills began to oppress her, now she was alone in them at night, and she grew still more tense, remembering a convincing detail about the hanged shepherd. As a child she'd been shown the actual branch used for the hanging: a tall branch, on which not a single leaf had grown, ever since. And she remembered, too, the pedlar, said to have been murdered higher up the valley in the year of Waterloo.

She'd come five miles. Now was the time to decide. Either she should press on, or she should turn off the track towards the glimmer of light coming from the cottage on the far side of the valley and tell Mr and Mrs Charlton. . . . Tell them *what*, though? She'd too much pride to say she was frightened, at her age. It was deeply comforting, nonetheless, to think that Mr Charlton would insist on seeing her home. He was, of course, very old. She was a lot more agile and probably stronger than he was and it wasn't fair of her to take him from his inglenook just because she was scared by the dark and some old story that was probably a pack of lies, anyhow. No. To claim Mr Charlton's help there had to be good, solid reasons. Since there weren't any, she had no choice. Nerving herself, she hurried the last three miles.

A drystone wall, four feet tall, its outline blacker than the night, marked the farm's boundary. Jean faltered in her step; halted. The wall looked different: an obstruction blocked the greater part of the gap through which the track ran. Approaching, breath suspended, she recognised with relief that the obstruction was only the Land Rover; then, just able to see how badly it was smashed, she was suddenly anxious again. Her father must have lost all control, to have rammed the wall at that angle, reducing two yards of it to a mound of rubble. He could be injured. Or worse.

Free of superstitious fear, Jean hurtled headlong to the farmhouse, choking with fears that were now all too real. As she ran, she shouted. Yet no one came hurrying out. More strangely still, not a dog barked.

As she drew near, the lights in the parlour and kitchen dimmed; then went out. Someone inside had extinguished the oil lamps. She lurched into the kitchen door, only to find it, as she'd never known it before, bolted firmly against her.

'Mum,' she cried, fists hammering, 'oh Mum, is Dad all right?'

Silence. Like a house of the dead.

'Do you hear? It's me, Mum. Why are the lights out? Oh, please somebody open the door. I don't know what's happening.'

Nothing stirred on the other side of the door. She beat madly upon it till the strength left her arms; then she rested her forehead against it and sobbed from weariness and bewilderment.

Suddenly she froze, hearing a movement behind her. A hand clamped the nape of her neck, held her a whole minute in a powerful grip, then jabbed her face painfully up against the door knocker.

'Well, girl, what's your name?'

Her spirit was up. 'Jean Grey. Where's my Mum? What's happened to my Dad? You're hurting me. Let *go*!'

'I want the truth out of you now,' the voice grated, 'so tell me. Are you on your own?'

She began railing again, wanting to know what was happening, but the hand thrust from behind, flattening her face against the door, stifling her protests.

'I'll ask just once more.' The accent was harsh,

unfamiliar, menacing. 'Are you sure you've brought no one along with you?'

The hand released its pressure on the back of her head and she nodded.

'Then round to the front with you,' the voice ordered.

She did as she was told, moved stumblingly on by painful jabs in the back from what, she realised with horror, could only be a gun. Her tormentor yanked her long hair behind to bring her to a halt at the parlour porch, before calling through the open door for lights.

Inside a spurt of flame was followed by a bluish blur as the wick of an oil lamp kindled, then yellowed to a glow that spread in a circle through the parlour. By the lamp, cigarette lighter still in his hand, stood a lank, dark-complexioned man, about her father's age. His left arm was in a dirty makeshift sling. As she watched, he dropped the lighter into his jacket pocket and picked up the revolver lying on the dresser next to the lamp. The spreading light revealed the tight-lipped, angry face of her mother, standing in the far corner of the room, clutching the hands of her brothers who stared stiffly up at her, their faces white with shock.

Jean rushed to her mother, sobbing, and clung to her. Her brothers, taking their cue from her, set up an uninhibited wailing.

'Mum,' she said, 'where are the dogs?'

Her mother's eyes flinched from hers. Jean looked hard at her mother's face, taut with strain, heard her strangulated breathing as she fought to keep control, and knew the answer, without a word spoken. Stooping to comfort her brothers, she saw something – a shape, a movement – in the tail of her eye. She came forward, dragged the tablecloth to one side, and found her father huddled beneath the table. He was gagged, feet and wrists lashed together with a length of rope secured at the end to a heavy table leg.

Her tears dried at their source. Her face whitened with rage. She swung round on the gunman with his arm in a sling and his accomplice – younger and massively built, with a crooked nose and menacing, fanatic eyes. It looked for all the world as if she'd rush them with flailing fists and feet.

'Jean!' Her mother's voice implored and warned at the same time. 'Don't, Jean. They'll kill you.'

Jean hesitated still.

'Come back here and stay next to me. Do as I say.'

Her mother's authority prevailed. Jean crossed to her, but continued to scowl venomously at their captors.

'And if it isn't the complete tomboy!' The lank one mocked, but with a hint of approval.

The other one said, with neither humour nor approval: 'If she knows what's good for her, she'll busy herself with women's work.'

'Sure and that's so, Ned,' the lank man agreed. 'I'm peckish myself, so let's hope her cooking's less poisonous than her looks. To make sure of which, you'd better step into the kitchen with the wee hellcat, while I see that no harm comes to the family in here.'

Ned, his revolver thrust into his belt beneath his jacket, watched in surly silence as Jean cooked a huge pot of porridge on the stove. Lanky, as she privately named his partner, twice looked in, either because he was bored keeping guard in the parlour or because he was hungry. The first time, he tilted upward his lean, dark features, sniffed and said: 'I tell you, she's a dab hand at the cooking.' On his second visit he couldn't resist bending over the porridge to watch its surface dimple and seethe as it cooked. 'I never yet saw so much porridge at a time. Is it to last a whole month, then?'

'There are other mouths to feed beside your own,' Jean answered, grim-faced and imitating her mother in a bad temper. She got her way, even serving her mother and brothers first. They wouldn't let her touch the rope binding her father, but she crouched at his head and fed him, mouthful by mouthful, from a bowl. He whispered back at her to say he wasn't hurt, and that she must take care and not provoke their visitors. They'd come from the north during the afternoon, taken the Land Rover, driven it madly down the track and wrecked it. Then they'd come back.

As the evening wore on, she made mugs of tea, washed dishes, scoured the pot and, with Ned looming always at her back, brought pillows and blankets from the bedrooms. These chores kept her so busy that she discovered in herself a relaxation of the acute tension and sense of danger she'd originally felt. She was shocked at herself when, for seconds at a time, she actually forgot her circumstances – even forgot the questions she tormented herself with, asking who these men could be and why they'd come here.

These questions were to be publicly answered when, at ten o'clock, Ned made everyone sit quietly in the parlour for what he called 'a wee entertainment'. This was provided by the BBC radio news; more particularly, by the report on two terrorists believed responsible for a pub bombing in Liverpool, involving several fatalities. They had travelled north in a stolen car, probably heading for the port of Stranraer, and had narrowly escaped falling into a police trap set for them near Gretna. One of them was thought to have been wounded. The terrorists could now be making for Leith or Berwick, since a broken-down car, possibly abandoned by them, had been found early that morning just off the A698, a few miles east of Hawick. The public were asked to give all information they might have direct to the police, and warned not to attempt independent action against men who could well be desperate and were known to be murderers.

Ned shut the radio off the second it switched to another news item.

'That's not nice language at all to be using in front of the children,' Lanky mock-protested, clicking his tongue at the impropriety. But George sat fidgeting with his feet. He hadn't understood, and Alec, up beyond his bedtime, slept in a huddle beside his mother.

'Still, it's a real pity you haven't television. You need

electricity for that. And haven't you a mind to see yourself on the coloured screen, Ned?'

Ned said nothing. His eyes smouldered nastily above the crooked nose.

Jean watched her mother, who sat rigid on the edge of the sofa, swallowing hard on her anger and the fear she felt for the family; not to be drawn. She could hardly bear to look towards her father, to witness his helplessness, bound hand and foot under the table, but she was aware of his eyes searching for hers, as if trying to strengthen and reassure her.

Finally, her mother spoke, her voice metallic: 'Why don't you just go? They'll catch you once you stop moving.'

'So the statue can speak, can it?' Lanky exclaimed. 'Well now, I'll tell you. You arrange the transport and we'll be on our way quick enough. But till the taxi comes, we'll just have to impose on your hospitality while my arm convalesces a bit. And besides, if I had the free choice, wouldn't I as soon have the lot of you for hostages as the Royal Family itself? The forces of law and order surely don't crawl about here, at the back of beyond; and if they do, I reckon our necks aren't at risk so long as you're all around to put in a good word for us murderers by saying you're still alive. That is, if you behave yourselves and *are* still alive.'

Superficially, Lanky was much more companionable and human than his physically aggressive partner. But Jean wasn't taken in by this. He gave the orders. His unrelenting banter was embittered by some twist of nature. He was a man who'd risk everything for the excellent reason that nothing held any meaning for him. If the police stormed the place, he'd kill his hostages with mock apologies. But if he were to move out now, into the night, taking Ned with him, mightn't he kill them all anyhow, to ensure their silence?

With the realisation of this came a sudden hardening of purpose. To challenge a man who'd stop at nothing, she'd have to stop at nothing herself; be willing to risk everything, if need be. It's what her mother wouldn't dare do, out of fear for the children. It's what her father *would* do, but couldn't, tied like a bundle beneath the table. It was one thing, however, to feel the resolution harden inside her; quite another to know what action to take. All that was clear to her was that she must somehow escape and bring help.

The night was turning cold. She was on the point of suggesting a fire, hoping they'd let her outside, to fetch wood. She might find a way of breaking from Ned in the dark, though there'd be little chance of that, since he'd very likely twist a hunk of her long hair round his hand, as he'd done following her upstairs for blankets. And what if she *did* escape? Mightn't they kill everyone, before moving out? Hadn't she already decided they'd be capable of that?

A shiver ran through her. Instinctively, she looked at the great stone fireplace and ingle, big enough to sit two on either side. If you poked your head directly under the chimney, you could see foot-ledges used long ago by boy chimney sweepers. Lanky was talking again, but she heard not a word he said. The door was locked, its key in Lanky's pocket; the sash windows were heavy, creaky, their latches noticeable, if undone. . . .

Suddenly she was praying that no one would ask for a fire! Because she saw now precisely what she must do. Not just how to escape and save her own skin, but much more – like how to creep back with the means to give her father the revenge she knew he was desperate to take. Her plan had come to her entire and she caught her breath with excitement.

Announcing it was time for bed, she helped her mother spread out cushions from the sofa and chairs, and covered her father with a blanket. Alec was left to sleep, but she went off to wash George, pursued by Ned, who stationed himself outside the bathroom door. Before emerging, she used a razor blade to cut off two thick strands of her long, light-coloured hair and slipped them into the pocket of her school blazer; then, to avoid detection, she tied the rest of her hair in an untidy, loose bun. Presently she was breathing steadily, pretending sleep, and taking care to pull the blanket well over her head. As she did so, she thought tearfully of the dogs; then she concentrated on the details of her plan.

As before, Ned kept to the kitchen and would be slumped in the windsor chair he'd placed up against the back door. Lanky sat at the parlour table, but was restless, perhaps from the pain of his wound. After half an hour he went along to the kitchen to mumble with Ned and Jean was tempted to put her plan into action, but suspected it could bc premature: rightly, as it turned out, for the next minute he came back and moved right round the parlour, taking a long look at each of them. Then he turned the oil lamp low on the dresser and, reseating himself, rested his arm on the table.

Nothing stirred in the room for two hours, except the agile thoughts of those awake: her father, her mother, Lanky and herself. At last, Jean felt the tiredness working in her body like a drug and lay in terror of falling asleep, despite herself. Then Lanky moved, stood up, shadow-like, and drew in his breath sharply, from pain. He would go through to Ned, now, to have his wound looked at, or at least to seek relief from it in talk.

Jean was scrambling from her blankets almost before he was out of the door. Snatching a pillow and spare cushions she'd left within reach, she drew the blankets over them, shaping them to resemble a body. Where the blanket was pulled over the supposed head (a small cushion), she thrust the strands of her hair, leaving the ends, no more than three inches, visibly exposed. Her mother sat up, staring at her, making sibilant whispers. Jean raised a warning finger and whispered back: 'Don't worry, I'll get help.' Leaning towards the table, she repeated to her father: 'Don't worry.'

She stooped, then stood upright in the chimney and groped blindly to locate foot-ledges that hadn't felt the pressure of a foot in more than a century. Yet they held, miraculously as it seemed to her. Only caked soot flaked from the brickwork as she moved upward, at first with plenty of shoulder room, then with progressively less as her head came level with the fireplace of the dark bedroom above: her parents' room. She had to back down the chimney and begin again, this time ascending with hands held over her head, like someone about to take a dive. This way, her hands could grip the strong ironwork of the grate, and with this for purchase, she eased herself from the chimney into the fireplace and so into the room. She crossed and opened the casement window, then, seizing the sheets from the bed, knotted them and looped one end round the window itself, which, as she lowered herself to within an easy drop to the ground, bit hard into the linen, but made no sound.

Safe on the fringe of lawn outside, within a foot of the parlour window, hardly brighter than the starry night overhead, Jean paused a while, trying to distinguish above the pounding of her heart any sound that might indicate she'd been missed. Not a mouse stirred. She edged to the corner nearest the kitchen and could just make out a murmurous monotone that could only be Lanky talking. With eyes still not quite used to the dark, she moved towards the back of the house, but very nearly pitched headlong over something that shouldn't have been there. But before her hand reached out and actually touched the shaggy, cold coat, she knew it was Belle. Not two yards away was a huddled shadow that had once been Beau.

She felt no impulse to weep. Only a new fearlessness; a blinding belief that nothing could now deflect her, that failure was impossible.

Jean made her way cautiously to the rear stone wall, mounted the stile, pausing for the last time to listen to the total silence all around her, then quickly jumped down and took the steepest path up the great shadowy hill behind the farmhouse, half running and half scrambling to get clear of impeding heather and bracken and climb the higher reaches of short, wind-bitten grass where her father's sheep grazed by day. Disturbed by her, a few sheep lying in her path shot to their feet and ran off into the night, bleating; then suddenly stopped short, standing stock still.

Ignoring the mountainous roughness of the terrain, Mr Rutherford's farm, The Dykes, lay four miles to the east, in the next valley but one. Jean kept the pace of a hardened fell-runner, her determination too fierce to let her limbs tire or slacken. On the far side of the first hill, her legs ran away with her, so that she had to fling herself flat on her back, spread-eagled, hands frantically pawing the slope, to stop the headlong hirpling that could have broken her neck. On across the valley, through squelchy marsh and reeds, then again up and up the steepening shoulder of the next hill, with sky and stars jogging and staggering crazily overhead. She fell, cutting hands and legs on scree that slid like treacherous ice under her feet, but felt nothing. On her left the vast outline of The Cheviot rose like a black whale humped against the sky. In her veins was an excitement that seemed to propel her forwards and up, to the second, higher summit. As she ran she could feel her heart leaping wildly within her and in her exhilaration it was as if all the dead past of her English lessons came alive, so that for the first time she knew the reality of feud and murder and tragic love. They'd been as alive as she now was, all those ancestors of hers – all those villains in the ballads; all those revenging heroes and ladies combing yellow hair, unafraid of death or demon lovers – and were of the same flesh and blood as herself. They'd been held in the grip of the same exaltation that held her now. They half seemed to be at her side, keeping pace with her, step by step as she ran.

Within a bare half hour of setting out, she was shouting with all the breath left in her as she came down to the flat meadowland surrounding The Dykes. Immediately, the dogs, well known to her, set up an answering clamour, but kept to the farmyard until she drew nearer. A weak light grew gradually in an upstairs bedroom and by the time she'd reached the front gate, with the dogs leaping excitedly about her, Mr Rutherford's head was thrust through the window, wanting to know who was there.

'Jean Grey,' she called up. 'We need your help, Mr Rutherford.'

He wasted no time in giving it. Ten minutes later she was drinking hot milk laced with brandy in the kitchen. While attending to her, Mrs Rutherford, her husband's greatcoat pulled over her nightdress, praised Jean to her face, stopping only to chivvy Bill, in pyjamas, to be quicker about it with hot water, soap, TCP, plasters, blankets, basins; an endless list of wants. He scampered round out of desperate concern for Jean, at the same time hating his mother for ordering him about in front of her like that.

Not that Jean noticed. Her attention was strained to hear Mr Rutherford, who was in the hall, phoning the Berwick police. She could hear just enough to have her fears confirmed. The police were insisting on taking over entirely. They rejected her plan out of hand, as Mr Rutherford said they would. He was told to keep her safely at The Dykes while they organised an operation to besiege Higham Farm.

When he'd finished, Mr Rutherford drew up a chair facing her and repeated it all, trying not to hurt her feelings. 'Ye must see, Jeannie,' he said finally, persuasively, 'that the police wouldna dare allow a young lassie – I mean a minor – to take such a risk. It's very brave of ye, but they wouldna agree, ever. They've got their duty to do.'

'It's my plan and I *know* it can't fail,' Jean insisted, voice low but intense. 'I also know who I have to deal with, better than the police. When they see the police closing in on them they'll kill everybody. Because of me. Then I'll kill myself. Then the police will have done their duty.' As she spoke, her eyes, deadly serious, never wavered from his.

'Jeannie, Jeannie!' Mr Rutherford protested, though visibly uneasy.

'The lassie could be in the right of it,' Mrs Rutherford said, playing on his uncertainty. 'Ye'd be hard put to it to fault her plan so far as it's gone.'

'Ay, but it's too late now. They know it all, so it's out of our hands. I'm sorry, lassie, but it canna be mended now. Ye'll have to bide here and get some sleep.'

'It *has* to be my plan. How do you think I could sleep? And what will you say, waking me to tell me they've murdered my Mam and my Dad and my two brothers?' Her voice was hard, dry; without tears.

Mr Rutherford recognised a will more powerful than his own. 'Ye're not much more than a bairn,' he said, and shot angrily to his feet. 'Ye'll just have to do as ye're told.'

Jean set her face at him, hard-jawed, unflinching.

'You can't make her give in, father,' Bill said, face flushed.

But it was left to Mrs Rutherford to tip the scales. 'Well, Geordie lad,' – voice neutral, matter-of-fact – 'as I've said, the lassie's plan has worked fine so far. I'll only say this, and shut up: I hope you wouldn't want it abandoned because it puts *you* in a wee bit of danger.'

That settled it. 'Get the gun,' he said quietly, with a glance at Bill. 'So ye've got your way, wife. Now see to it ye phone and tell them. They know weel enough what the lassie planned, so tell them the plan's going through. And warn them not to come within five miles of the place until it's daylight.'

Bill handed him rifle and cartridges. 'Please, father, I'll do anything.'

'Ay, so ye'll stay and look after your mother. Come then, Jeannie, we'll try what your plan's worth.'

'Aren't we forgetting the knife?' Jean asked.

They collected it from the kitchen drawer, went out into the dark, and were soon climbing, doubling back on Jean's tracks across the hills. The humped skyline of The Cheviot, now on their right, was just perceptibly a shade lighter, though it would be more than two hours to dawn. Twice they disturbed sleeping peewits, that flapped into the dark with alarmed weet-weetings, and the odd sheep went yammering away as, at last, they moved down to the farm.

They rested at the stile, catching their breath, watching the sleeping house not three hundred yards below. So far as Jean could tell, not a thing was different. Except . . . except for the sound of furtive movements higher up the hillside. Mr Rutherford laid a hand on her arm, listening, and took a firmer grip on the rifle.

The shadow bearing down on them took substance and halted a few feet away.

'Ay,' Mr Rutherford hissed, 'it's us, right enough. And I've a mind to flay the hide off ye for leaving your mother. We'll see later about that. Meanwhile, since ye're here, ye'll come along with me.'

Bill, trousers and jacket drawn over his pyjamas, following his father's example, moved closer and said nothing.

'Are ye completely sure, Jeannie?' Mr Rutherford turned on her.

'Could I have the gun, now? And the knife?'

He handed them over. 'Wrap the cartridges in this hanky and jam them deep in your pocket,' he said. Then: 'There's no shame at all in ye changing your mind, Jeannie. Are ye fair set on it?'

'More than anything in the world.' She sounded firm, confident.

'Ay. Then dinna forget to bide your time for the signal. The horn first, if it's working. Ye'll on no account move till we've caused a distraction. Now will ye abide by this?'

'You know I will, Mr Rutherford. It's part of the plan.'

'Weel now, we'll be off. I'll do my part, rest assured. Moreover, I'll pray for ye, Jeannie, though I'm not a praying man.' He gripped her arm, almost painfully, before moving quickly away.

'Take care,' Bill muttered, following his father into the night.

They'd reach the wrecked Land Rover in under ten minutes. Jean bound the sheathed knife to the rifle butt with string, leaving the ends dangling; then impatiently waited, never shifting her gaze from the dimly glowing parlour window on the other side of the freestone dyke. In the immense silence, she could hear the soft trickling of a nearby beck.

'Now,' she kept murmuring to herself, 'let it be now!'

Abruptly, the high-pitched, unmodulating blare of a motor-horn, loud even at a distance, pierced the silence and seemed to fill the whole valley. Dropping over the stile, she moved quickly, but without running, and within fifty yards of the house saw the first coiling leap of flame on her left. They'd wasted no time in getting at the spare can of petrol kept in the back of the Land Rover. And the kitchen window offered a grandstand view!

Passing close by the dark mounds that had been Border collies, mother and son, she gained the parlour wall, tied the dangling string binding the rifle and knife to the suspended sheet, and having hauled herself up to the casement with it, drew it up after her and untied the weapons. Stepping backwards into the fireplace, she lowered herself into the chimney, groping with knees and feet for foot-ledges, then eased herself down, lower and lower, with the rifle held high over her head. Her feet touched the ash of the fireplace beneath. For a second, she crouched there. Then her mother was beside her, helping her into the room, and endlessly repeating: 'Thank God! Oh, thank God!'

'Where are they, Mam?'

'Through in the kitchen. Or out the back. I heard them unbolt the door.'

She drew the knife from its sheath and thrust the rifle and cartridges on her mother. 'You load it, Mam. Quickly.'

Then she shot on all fours under the table to cut her

father free and peel off the gag, gabbling meanwhile about the diversion Mr Rutherford and Bill were creating at the back, outside.

Her father hugged her, without speaking, and struggled stiffly from under the table, easing himself erect and rubbing arms, legs, neck, to get the circulation moving. It was all exactly as she'd known, beyond all doubt, it would be. With the gun in her father's hands, her plan would have worked to perfection.

Her mother was on the very point of reaching across the rifle when Lanky, who had been drawn to the kitchen window by the blazing tongues of fire, came quickly down the passage and kicked open the door.

'Drop it!' he hissed, lurching into the centre of the room, his revolver pointed straight at her father. Very slowly, her mother lowered the rifle to the floor, and all Jean's exaltation seemed to sink with it.

'I thought I heard a commotion,' Lanky mocked, planting one foot on the rifle. Then: 'Hello, what's this, then?' His eyes took in Jean's smudged face, arms, legs, then veered towards the heaped blankets and protruding strands of hair. 'By Jesus,' he muttered, 'I do believe. . . .'

Jean ran sobbing to her father, clutching him.

'If you care about the lassie,' Lanky said evenly to her mother, 'you'll tell her to keep clear of her father. Else the one bullet might do for the two of them.'

'Come away, Jean.' Her mother's voice was faint with fear.

She did. But before breaking from him to stumble on the blankets, she slipped her father the knife. Lanky's eyes flinched instinctively aside at her as she pitched headlong to the floor. In the same second her father leapt, struck the revolver to the floor and lodged the point of the knife at Lanky's throat.

'Budge or speak and I'll cut the throat of you,' her

father growled, his voice low and deep with menace. 'Reach me the revolver, Jean. . . . And the rifle to your mother. . . . Now then – gag and ropes.'

It took two minutes to tie and bundle Lanky under the table. Then her father crossed to the window, unlatched it and heaved it up on its sashes. 'Now, Meg, wake the bairns and off with you all to the far side of the dyke. Keep out of sight and you'll be safe enough on this side of the house. You, too, Jean,' he added, 'you'll take no more risks this night.'

Jean was keeping watch by the door that led to the kitchen down the dark passage. 'Can I keep guard? Just till they've got through the window.'

'Ay, and not a second more.'

Her mother climbed out of the window, followed by George. It was while her father was lifting Alec, still asleep, through to his mother, that Jean heard footsteps. '*Dad!*' she warned.

He moved swifter than a shadow, pressing himself and her flat against the wall behind the opening door.

Ned pushed his way heavily into the room and stood for a second, trying to take in what was happening. Suddenly the barrel of the rifle jabbed the nape of his neck.

'Get his gun, Jean.'

When she'd taken it from his slack fingers, her father asked for extra rope. 'This one'll take more parcelling,' he said, dourly.

'What about Mr Rutherford?' Jean asked, once Ned was reunited with Lanky, under the table.

Her father was adjusting the wick of the oil lamp to get more light. 'First go and help your Mam bring the bairns back. Then put the kettle on in the kitchen. Then take that revolver – mind how you carry it! – to Mr Rutherford as a present from me and say we'd appreciate it if he and the lad would step by for an early morning cup of tea. If, that is, they can stop playing bonfires out there!'

When she was on the point of setting off, her father

delayed her a second, calling over to her, suddenly very serious. 'Did I tell you I'm proud of you, lassie? And so would your ancestors be. If you'd lived in times gone by, my Jeannie, they'd have made a fine ballad about your adventure this night.'

A TERRIBLY STRANGE BED

William Wilkie Collins

Shortly after my education at college was finished I happened to be staying in Paris with an English friend. We were both young men then, and lived, I am afraid, rather a wild life in the delightful city of our sojourn. One night we were idling about the neighbourhood of the Palais Royal, doubtful to what amusement we should next betake ourselves. My friend proposed a visit to Frascati's; but his suggestion was not to my taste. I knew Frascati's, as the French saying is, by heart; had lost and won plenty of five-franc pieces there, merely for amusement's sake, until it was amusement no longer, and was thoroughly tired, in fact, of all the ghastly respectabilities of such a social anomaly as a respectable gambling-house.

'For heaven's sake,' said I to my friend, 'let us go

somewhere where we can see a little genuine, blackguard, poverty-stricken gaming, with no false gingerbread glitter thrown over it at all. Let us get away from fashionable Frascati's, to a house where they don't mind letting in a man with a ragged coat, or a man with no coat, ragged or otherwise.'

'Very well,' said my friend, 'we needn't go out of the Palais Royal to find the sort of company you want. Here's the place just before us, as blackguard a place, by all report, as you could possibly wish to see.' In another minute we arrived at the door and entered the house.

When we got upstairs, and had left our hats and sticks with the door-keeper, we were admitted into the chief gambling-room. We did not find many people assembled there. But, few as the men were who looked up at us on our entrance, they were all types – lamentably true types – of their respective classes.

We had come to see blackguards; but these men were something worse. There is a comic side, more or less appreciable, in all 'blackguardism' – here there was nothing but tragedy – mute, weird tragedy. The quiet in the room was horrible. The thin, haggard, long-haired young man, whose sunken eyes fiercely watched the turning up of the cards, never spoke; the flabby, fat-faced, pimply player, who pricked his piece of pasteboard perseveringly to register how often black won and how often red – never spoke; the dirty, wrinkled old man, with the vulture eyes and the darned great-coat, who had lost his last sou, and still looked on desperately after he could play no longer – never spoke. Even the voice of the croupier sounded as if it were strangely dulled and thickened in the atmosphere of the room.

I had entered the place to laugh, but the spectacle before me was something to weep over. I soon found it necessary to take refuge in excitement from the depression of spirits which was fast stealing on me. Unfortunately I sought the nearest excitement by going to the table and beginning to play. Still more unfortunately, as the event will show, I won – won prodigiously, won incredibly; won at such a rate that the regular players at the table crowded round me; and, staring at my stakes with hungry, superstitious eyes, whispered to one another that the English stranger was going to break the bank.

The game was *rouge-et-noir.* I had played at it in every city in Europe, without, however, the care or the wish to study the 'theory of chances' – that philosopher's stone of all gamblers! And a gambler, in the strict sense of the word, I had never been.

But on this occasion it was very different – now, for the first time in my life, I felt what the passion for play really was. My success first bewildered, and then, in the most literal meaning of the word, intoxicated me. Incredible as it may appear, it is nevertheless true, that I only lost when I attempted to estimate chances, and played according to previous calculation. If I left everything to luck, and staked without any care or consideration, I was sure to win – to win in the face of every recognised probability in favour of the bank. At first, some of the men present ventured their money safely enough on my colour; but I speedily increased my stakes to sums which they dared not risk. One after another they left off playing, and breathlessly looked on at my game.

Still, time after time, I staked higher and higher, and still won. The excitement in the room rose to fever pitch. The silence was interrupted by a deep-muttered chorus of oaths and exclamations in different languages every time the gold was shovelled across to my side of the table – even the imperturbable croupier dashed his rake on the floor in a fury of astonishment at my success. But one man present preserved his self-possession, and that man was my friend. He came to my side, and, whispering in English, begged me to leave the place, satisfied with what I had already gained. I must do him the justice to say that he repeated his warnings and entreaties several times, and only left me and went away after I had rejected his advice (I was to all intents and purposes gambling-drunk) in terms which rendered it impossible for him to address me again that night.

Shortly after he had gone a hoarse voice behind me cried, 'Permit me, my dear sir! – permit me to restore to their proper place two Napoleons which you have dropped. Wonderful luck, sir! I pledge you my word of honour, as an old soldier, in the course of my long experience in this sort of thing, I never saw such luck as yours! – never! Go on, sir – *sacré mille bombes!* Go on boldly, and break the bank!'

I turned round and saw, nodding and smiling at me with inveterate civility, a tall man, dressed in a frogged and braided coat.

If I had been in my senses I should have considered him, personally, as being rather a suspicious specimen of an old soldier. He had goggling bloodshot eyes, mangy mustachios, and a broken nose. His voice betrayed a barrack-room intonation of the worst order, and he had the dirtiest pair of hands I ever saw – even in France. These little personal peculiarities exercised, however, no repelling influence on me. In the mad excitement, the reckless triumph of that moment, I was ready to 'fraternise' with anybody who encouraged me in my game. I accepted the old soldier's offered pinch of snuff, clapped him on the back, and swore he was the most honest fellow in the world, the most glorious relic of the Grand Army that I had ever met with. 'Go on!' cried my military friend, snapping his fingers in ecstasy. 'Go on, and win! Break the bank – *mille tonnerres!* my gallant English comrade, break the bank!'

And I *did* go on – went on at such a rate that in another quarter of an hour the croupier called out, 'Gentlemen! The bank has discontinued for tonight.' All the notes and all the gold in that 'bank' now lay in a heap under my hands; the whole floating capital of the gambling-house was waiting to pour into my pockets!

'Tie up the money in your pocket-handkerchief, my worthy sir,' said the old soldier, as I wildly plunged my hands into my heap of gold. 'Tie it up, as we used to tie up a bit of dinner in the Grand Army; your winnings are too heavy for any breeches pockets that ever were sewed. There, that's it! Shovel them in, notes and all! And now, as an ancient grenadier, as an ex-brave of the French Army, what remains for me to do! I ask what? Simply this: to entreat my valued English friend to drink a bottle of champagne with me, and toast the goddess fortune in foaming goblets before we part!'

'Excellent ex-brave! Convivial ancient grenadier! Champagne by all means! An English cheer for an old soldier!'

'Bravo! the Englishman; the amiable, gracious Englishman, in whose veins circulates the vivacious blood of France! Another glass? Ah – the bottle is empty! Never mind! *Vive le vin!* I, the old soldier, order another bottle!'

'No, no, ex-brave; never – ancient grenadier! *Your* bottle last time, *my* bottle this. Behold it! Toast away! The French Army! – The great Napoleon! – The present company! The croupier! The honest croupier's wife and daughters – if he has any! The ladies generally! Everybody in the world!'

By this time the second bottle of champagne was emptied. I felt as if I had been drinking liquid fire – my brain seemed all aflame. No excess in wine had ever had this effect on me before in my life. Was it the result of a stimulant acting upon my system when I was in a highly excited state? Was my stomach in a particularly disordered condition? Or was the champagne amazingly strong?

'Ex-brave of the French Army!' cried I, in a mad state of exhilaration, '*I* am on fire! how are *you*? You have set me on fire! Do you hear, my hero of Austerlitz? Let us have a third bottle to put the flame out!'

The old soldier wagged his head, rolled his goggle eyes, until I expected to see them slip out of their sockets; placed his dirty forefinger by the side of his broken nose, solemnly ejaculated, 'Coffee!' and immediately ran off into an inner room.

The word pronounced by the eccentric veteran seemed to have a magical effect on the rest of the company present. With one accord they all rose to depart. Probably they had expected to profit by my intoxication; but finding that my new friend was benevolently bent on preventing me from getting dead drunk, had now abandoned all hope of thriving pleasantly on my winnings. Whatever their motive might be, at any rate they went away in a body. When the old soldier returned and sat down again opposite to me at the table, we had the room to ourselves. I could see the croupier, in a sort of vestibule which opened out of it, eating his supper in solitude. The silence was now deeper than ever.

A sudden change, too, had come over the 'ex-brave'. He assumed a portentously solemn look, and when he spoke to me again his speech was ornamented by no oaths, enforced by no finger-snapping, enlivened by no apostrophes or exclamations.

'Listen, my dear sir,' said he, in mysteriously confidential tones, 'listen to an old soldier's advice. I have been to the mistress of the house – a very charming woman, with a genius for cookery! – to impress on her the necessity of making us some particularly strong and good coffee. You must drink this coffee in order to get rid of your little amiable exaltation of spirits before you think of going home – you *must*, my good and gracious friend! With all that money to take home tonight, it is a sacred duty to yourself to have your wits about you. You are known to be a winner to an enormous extent by several gentlemen present tonight, who, in a certain point of view, are very worthy and excellent fellows; but they are mortal men, my dear sir, and they have their amiable weaknesses! Need I say more? Ah, no, no! you understand me! Now, this is what you must do. Send for a cabriolet when you feel quite well again, draw up all the windows when you get into it, and tell the driver to take you home only through the large and well-lit thoroughfares. Do this, and you and your money will be safe. Do this, and tomorrow you will thank an old soldier for giving you a word of honest advice.'

Just as the ex-brave ended his oration in very lugubrious tones, the coffee came in, ready poured out in two cups. My attentive friend handed me one of the cups with a bow. I was parched with thirst, and drank it off at a draught. Almost instantly afterwards I was seized with a fit of giddiness, and felt more completely intoxicated than ever. The room whirled round and round furiously; the old soldier seemed to be regularly bobbing up and down before me like the piston of a steam-engine. I was half deafened by a violent singing in my ears; a feeling of utter bewilderment, helplessness, idiocy overcame me. I rose from my chair, holding on by the table to keep my balance, and stammered out that I felt dreadfully unwell, so unwell that I did not know how I was to get home.

'My dear friend,' answered the old soldier – and even his voice seemed to be bobbing up and down as he spoke – 'my dear friend, it would be madness to go home in *your* state; you would be sure to lose your money; you might be robbed and murdered with the greatest ease. *I* am going to sleep here: *you* sleep here, too – they make up capital beds in this house – take one; sleep off the effects of the wine, and go home safely with your winnings tomorrow – tomorrow, in broad daylight.'

I had but two ideas left: one, that I must never let go hold of my handkerchief full of money; the other, that I must lie down somewhere immediately and fall off into a comfortable sleep. So I agreed to the proposal about the bed, and took the offered arm of the old soldier, carrying my money with my disengaged hand. Preceded by the croupier, we passed along some passages and up a flight of stairs into the bedroom which I was to occupy. The ex-brave shook me warmly by the hand, proposed that we should breakfast together, and then, followed by the croupier, left me for the night.

I ran to the wash-stand, drank some of the water in my jug, poured the rest out, and plunged my face into it, then sat down in a chair and tried to compose myself. I soon felt better. The change for my lungs from the stinking atmosphere of the gambling-room to the cool air of the apartment I now occupied; the almost equally refreshing change for my eyes from the glaring gaslights of the salon to the dim, quiet flicker of one bedroom candle, aided wonderfully the restorative effects of cold water. The giddiness left me, and I began to feel a little like a reasonable being again. My first thought was of the risk of sleeping all night in a gambling-house; my second, of the still greater risk of trying to get out after the house was closed, and of going home alone at night, through the streets of Paris, with a large sum of money about me. I had slept in worse places than this on my travels; so I determined to lock, bolt, and barricade my door, and take my chance till the next morning.

Accordingly, I secured myself against all intrusion, looked under the bed and into the cupboard, tried the fastening of the window, and then, satisfied that I had taken every proper precaution, pulled off my upper clothing, put my light, which was a dim one, on the hearth among a feathery litter of wood ashes, and got into bed, with the handkerchief full of money under my pillow.

I soon felt not only that I could not go to sleep, but that I could not even close my eyes. I was wide awake, and in a high fever. Every nerve in my body trembled – every one of my senses seemed to be preternaturally sharpened.

What could I do? I had no book to read. I raised myself on my elbow, and looked about the room, which was brightened by a lovely moonlight pouring straight through the window – to see if it contained any pictures or ornaments that I could at all clearly distinguish.

There was, first, the bed I was lying in; a four-post

bed, of all things in the world to meet with in Paris! – yes, a thorough clumsy British four-poster, with the regular top lined with chintz – the regular fringed valance all round – the regular stifling unwholesome curtains, which I remembered having mechanically drawn back against the posts without particularly noticing the bed when I first got into the room. Then there was the marble-topped wash-stand, from which the water I had spilt, in my hurry to pour it out, was still dripping, slowly and more slowly, on to the brick floor. Then two small chairs.

Then the window – an unusually large window. Then a dark old picture, which the feeble candle dimly showed me. It was the picture of a fellow in a high Spanish hat, crowned with a plume of towering feathers. A swarthy, sinister ruffian, looking upward, shading his eyes with his hand, and looking intently upward – it might be at some tall gallows at which he was going to be hanged. At any rate, he had the appearance of thoroughly deserving it.

This picture put a kind of constraint upon me to look upward too – at the top of the bed. It was a gloomy and not an interesting object, and I looked back at the picture. I counted the feathers in the man's hat – they stood out in relief – three white, two green. I observed the crown of his hat, which was of a conical shape, according to the fashion supposed to have been favoured by Guy Fawkes. I counted the feathers again – three white, two green.

While I still lingered over this very improving and intellectual employment, my thoughts insensibly began to wander. The moonlight shining into the room reminded me of a certain moonlight night in Britain – the night after a picnic party in a Welsh valley. Every incident of the drive homeward, through lovely scenery, which the moonlight made lovelier than ever, came back to me, though I had never given the picnic a thought for years; though, if I had *tried* to recollect it, I could certainly have recalled little or nothing of that scene long past.

I was still thinking of the picnic – of our merriment on the drive home – of the sentimental young lady who *would* quote *Childe Harold* because it was moonlight. I was absorbed by these past scenes and past amusements, when, in an instant, the thread on which my memories hung snapped asunder: my attention immediately came back to present things more vividly than ever, and I found myself, I neither knew why nor wherefore, looking hard at the picture again.

Looking for what?

Good God! the man had pulled his hat down on his brows! – No, the hat itself was gone! Where was the conical crown? Where the feathers – three white, two green? Not there! In place of the hat and feathers, what dusky object was it that now hid his forehead, his eyes, his shading hand?

Was the bed moving?

I turned on my back and looked up. Was I mad? Drunk? Dreaming? Giddy again? Or was the top of the bed really moving down – sinking slowly, regularly, silently, horribly, right down throughout the whole of its length and breadth – right down upon me as I lay underneath?

My blood seemed to stand still. A deadly paralysing coldness stole all over me as I turned my head round on the pillow and determined to test whether the bed-top was really moving or not by keeping my eye on the man in the picture.

The next look in that direction was enough. The dull, black, frowsy outline of the valance above me was within an inch of being parallel with his waist. I still looked breathlessly. And steadily, and slowly – very slowly – I saw the figure, and the line of frame below the figure, vanish as the valance moved down before it.

I am, constitutionally, anything but timid. I have been on more than one occasion in peril of my life, and have not lost my self-possession for an instant; but when the conviction first settled on my mind that the bed-top was really moving, was steadily and continuously sinking down upon me, I looked up shuddering, helpless, panic-stricken, beneath the hideous machinery for murder, which was advancing closer and closer to suffocate me where I lay.

I looked up, motionless, speechless, breathless. The candle, fully spent, went out; but the moonlight still brightened the room. Down and down, without pausing and without sounding, came the bed-top, and still my panic-terror seemed to bind me faster and faster to the mattress on which I lay – down and down it sank, till the dusty odour from the lining of the canopy came stealing into my nostrils.

At that final moment the instinct of self-preservation startled me out of my trance and I moved at last. There was just room for me to roll myself sideways off the bed. As I dropped noiselessly to the floor the edge of the murderous canopy touched me on the shoulder.

Without stopping to draw my breath, without wiping the cold sweat from my face, I rose instantly on my knees to watch the bed-top. I was literally spellbound by it. If I had heard footsteps behind me, I could not have turned round; if a means of escape had been miraculously provided for me, I could not have moved to take advantage of it. The whole life in me was, at that moment, concentrated in my eyes.

It descended – the whole canopy, with the fringe round it, came down – down – close down, so close that there was not room now to squeeze my finger between the bed-top and the bed. I felt at the sides, and discovered that what had appeared to me from beneath to be the ordinary light canopy of a four-post bed was in reality a thick, broad mattress, the substance of which was concealed by the valance and its fringe. I looked up and saw the four posts rising hideously bare. In the middle of the bed-top was a huge wooden screw that had evidently worked it down through a hole in the ceiling, just as ordinary presses are worked down on the substance selected for compression.

The frightful apparatus moved without making the

faintest noise. There had been no creaking as it came down; there was now not the faintest sound from the room above. Amid a dead and awful silence I beheld before me – in the nineteenth century, and in the civilised capital of France – such a machine for secret murder by suffocation as might have existed in the worst days of the Inquisition, in the lonely inns among the Hartz Mountains, in the mysterious tribunals of Westphalia! Still, as I looked on it I could not move, I could hardly breathe, but I began to recover the power of thinking, and in a moment I discovered the murderous conspiracy framed against me in all its horror. My cup of coffee had been drugged, and drugged too strongly. I had been saved from being smothered by having taken an overdose of some narcotic. How I had chafed and fretted at the fever-fit which had preserved my life by keeping me awake! How recklessly I had confided myself to the two wretches who had led me into this room, determined, for the sake of my winnings, to kill me in my sleep by the surest and most horrible contrivance for secretly accomplishing my destruction! How many men, winners like me, had slept, as I had proposed to sleep, in that bed and had never been seen or heard of more! I shuddered at the bare idea of it.

But ere long all thought was again suspended by the sight of the murderous canopy moving once more. After it had remained on the bed – as nearly as I could guess – about ten minutes, it began to move up again. The villains who worked it from above evidently believed that their purpose was now accomplished. Slowly and silently, as it had descended, that horrible bed-top rose towards its former place. When it reached the upper extremities of the four posts, it reached the ceiling too. Neither hole nor screw could be seen; the bed became in appearance an ordinary bed again – the canopy an ordinary canopy – even to the most suspicious eyes.

Now, for the first time, I was able to move – to rise

from my knees – to dress myself in my upper clothing – and to consider of how I should escape. If I betrayed, by the smallest noise, that the attempt to suffocate me had failed, I was certain to be murdered. Had I made any noise already? I listened intently, looking towards the door.

No! No footsteps in the passage outside – no sound of a tread, light or heavy, in the room above – absolute silence everywhere. Besides locking and bolting my door I had moved an old wooden chest against it, which I had found under the bed. To remove this chest (my blood ran cold as I thought of what its contents might be!) without making some disturbance was impossible: and, moreover, to think of escaping through the house, now barred up for the night, was sheer insanity. Only one chance was left me – the window. I stole to it on tiptoe.

My bedroom was on the first floor, above an *entresol*, and looked into the back street. I raised my hand to open the window, knowing that on that action hung, by the merest hair's-breath, my chance of safety. They keep vigilant watch in a house of murder. If any part of the frame cracked, if the hinge creaked, I was a lost man! It must have occupied me at least five minutes, reckoning by time – five *hours*, reckoning by suspense – to open that window. I succeeded in doing it silently – in doing it with all the dexterity of a house-breaker – and then looked down into the street. To leap the distance beneath me would be almost certain destruction! Next, I looked round at the sides of the house. Down the left side ran the thick water-pipe – it passed close by the outer edge of the window. The moment I saw the pipe I knew I was saved. My breath came and went freely for the first time since I had seen the canopy of the bed moving down upon me!

To some men the means of escape which I had discovered might have seemed difficult and dangerous enough – to *me* the prospect of slipping down the pipe into the street did not suggest even a thought of peril. I had always been accustomed, by the practice of gymnastics, to keep up my schoolboy powers as a daring and expert climber, and knew that my head, hands, and feet would serve me faithfully in any hazards of ascent or descent. I had already got one leg over the windowsill when I remembered the handkerchief filled with money under my pillow. I could well have afforded to leave it behind me, but I was revengefully determined that the miscreants of the gambling-house should miss their plunder as well as their victim.

So I went back to the bed and tied the heavy handkerchief at my back by my cravat. Just as I had made it tight and fixed it in a comfortable place, I thought I heard a sound of breathing outside the door. The chill feeling of horror ran through me again as I listened. No! dead silence still in the passage – I had heard the night air blowing softly into the room. The next moment I was on the windowsill – and the next I had a firm grip on the water-pipe with my hands and knees.

I slid down into the street easily and quietly, as I thought I should, and immediately set off at the top of my speed to a branch Prefecture of Police, which I knew was situated in the immediate neighbourhood. A Sub-prefect and several picked men among his subordinates happened to be up, maturing, I believe, some scheme for discovering the perpetrator of a mysterious murder which all Paris was talking of just then. When I began my story, in a breathless hurry and in very bad French, I could see that the Sub-prefect suspected me of being a drunken Englishman who had robbed somebody; but he soon altered his opinion as I went on, and before I had anything like concluded, he shoved all the papers before him into a drawer, put on his hat, supplied me with another (for I was bare-headed), ordered a file of soldiers, desired his expert followers to get ready all sorts of tools for breaking open doors and ripping up brick-flooring, and took my arm in the most friendly and familiar manner possible to lead me with him out of the house. I will venture to say that when the

Sub-prefect was a little boy, and was taken for the first time to the play, he was not half as much pleased as he was now at the job in prospect for him at the gambling-house!

Away we went through the streets, the Sub-prefect cross-examining and congratulating me in the same breath as we marched at the head of our formidable posse. Sentinels were placed at the back and front of the house the moment we got to it; a tremendous battery of knocks was directed against the door; a light appeared at a window; I was told to conceal myself behind the police – then came more knocks, and a cry of 'Open in the name of the law!' At that terrible summons bolts and locks gave way before an invisible hand, and the moment after the Sub-prefect was in the passage, confronting a waiter half-dressed and ghastly pale. This was the short dialogue which immediately took place:

'We want to see the Englishman who is sleeping in this house.'

'He went away hours ago.'

'He did no such thing. His friend went away; *he* remained. Show us to his bedroom!'

'I swear to you, *Monsieur le Sous-préfet*, he is not here! He—'

'I swear to you, *Monsieur le Garçon*, he is. He slept here – he didn't find your bed comfortable – he came to us to complain of it – here he is among my men – and here am I ready to look for a flea or two in his bedstead. Renaudin!' (calling to one of the subordinates and pointing to the waiter) 'collar that man and tie his hands behind him. Now, then, gentlemen, let us walk upstairs!'

Every man and woman in the house was secured – the 'old soldier' the first. Then I identified the bed in which I had slept, and then we went into the room above.

No object that was at all extraordinary appeared in any part of it. The Sub-prefect looked round the place, commanded everybody to be silent, stamped twice on the floor, called for a candle, looked attentively at the spot he had stamped on, and ordered the flooring there to be carefully taken up. This was done in no time. Lights were produced, and we saw a deep raftered cavity between the floor of this room and the ceiling of the room beneath. Through this cavity there ran perpendicularly a sort of case of iron thickly greased, and inside the case appeared the screw which communicated with the bed-top below. Extra lengths of screw, freshly oiled; levers covered with felt; all the complete upper works of a heavy press – constructed with infernal ingenuity so as to join the fixtures below, and when taken to pieces again to go into the smallest possible compass – were next discovered and pulled out on the floor. After some little difficulty the Sub-prefect succeeded in putting the machinery together, and, leaving his men to work it, descended with me to the bedroom. The smothering canopy was then lowered, but not so noiselessly as I had seen it lowered. When I mentioned this to the Sub-prefect, his answer, simple as it was, had a terrible significance. 'My men,' said he, 'are working down the bed-top for the first time – the men whose money you won were in better practice.'

We left the house in the sole possession of two police agents – every one of the inmates being removed to prison on the spot. The Sub-prefect, after taking down my statement in his office, returned with me to my hotel to get my passport. 'Do you think,' I asked as I gave it to him, 'that any men have really been smothered in that bed as they tried to smother *me*?'

'I have seen dozens of drowned men laid out at the morgue,' answered the Sub-prefect, 'in whose pocket-books were found letters stating that they had committed suicide in the Seine, because they had lost everything at the gaming-table. Do I know how many of those men entered the same gambling-house that *you* entered, won as *you* won, took that bed as you took it, slept in it, were smothered in it, and were privately thrown into the river with a letter of explanation written by the murderers and placed in their pocket-books? No man can say how many or how few have suffered the fate from which you have escaped. The people of the gambling-house kept their bedstead machinery a secret from *us* – even from the police! The dead kept the rest of the secret for them. Goodnight, or rather good-morning, Monsieur.'

One good result was produced by my adventure: it cured me of ever again trying *rouge-et-noir* as an amusement. The sight of a green cloth, with packs of cards and heaps of money on it, will henceforth be forever associated in my mind with the sight of a bed-canopy descending to suffocate me in the silence and darkness of the night.

IN THE ABYSS

H. G. Wells

The lieutenant stood in front of the steel sphere and gnawed a piece of pine splinter. 'What do you think of it, Steevens?' he asked.

'It's an idea,' said Steevens, in the tone of one who keeps an open mind.

'I believe it will smash – flat,' said the lieutenant.

'He seems to have calculated it all out pretty well,' said Steevens, still impartial.

'But think of the pressure,' said the lieutenant. 'At the surface of the water it's fourteen pounds to the inch, thirty feet down it's double that; sixty, treble, ninety, four times; nine hundred, forty times; five thousand, three hundred – that's a mile – it's two hundred and forty times fourteen pounds; that's – let's see – thirty hundredweight – a ton and half, Steevens; *a ton and a half* to the square inch. And the ocean where he's going is five miles deep. That's seven and a half—'

'Sounds a lot,' said Steevens, 'but it's jolly thick steel.'

The lieutenant made no answer, but resumed his pine splinter. The object of their conversation was a huge ball of steel, having an exterior diameter of perhaps nine feet. It looked like the shot for some Titanic piece of artillery. It was elaborately nested in a monstrous scaffolding built into the framework of the vessel, and the gigantic spars that were presently to sling it overboard gave the stern of the ship an appearance that had raised the curiosity of every decent sailor who had sighted it, from the Pool of London to the Tropic of Capricorn. In two places, one above the other, the steel gave place to a couple of circular windows of enormously thick glass, and one of these, set in a steel frame of great solidity, was now partially unscrewed. Both the men had seen the interior of this globe for the first time that morning. It was elaborately padded with air cushions, with little studs sunk between bulging pillows to work the simple mechanism of the affair. Everything was elaborately padded, even the Meyers apparatus which was to absorb carbonic acid and replace the oxygen inspired by its tenant, when he had crept in by the glass manhole, and had been screwed in. It was so elaborately padded that a man might have been fired from a gun in it with perfect safety. And it had need to be, for presently a man was to crawl in through that glass manhole, to be screwed up tightly, and to be flung overboard, and to sink down – down – down, for five miles, even as the lieutenant said. It had taken the strongest hold of his imagination; it made him a bore at mess; and he found Steevens, the new arrival aboard, a godsend to talk to about it, over and over again.

'It's my opinion,' said the lieutenant, 'that that glass will simply bend in and bulge and smash, under a pressure of that sort. Daubrée has made rocks run like water under big pressures – and, you mark my words—'

'If the glass did break in,' said Steevens, 'what then?'

'The water would shoot in like a jet of iron. Have you ever felt a straight jet of high-pressure water? It would hit as hard as a bullet. It would simply smash him and flatten him. It would tear down his throat, and into his lungs; it would blow in his ears—'

'What a detailed imagination you have!' protested Steevens, who saw things vividly.

'It's a simple statement of the inevitable,' said the lieutenant.

'And the globe?'

'Would just give out a few little bubbles, and it would settle down comfortably against the day of judgement, among the oozes and the bottom clay – with poor Elstead spread over his own smashed cushions like butter over bread.'

He repeated this sentence as though he liked it very much. 'Like butter over bread,' he said.

'Having a look at the jigger?' said a voice, and Elstead stood between them, spick and span in white, with a cigarette between his teeth, and his eyes smiling out of the shadow of his ample hat-brim. 'What's that about bread and butter, Weybridge? Grumbling as usual about the insufficient pay of naval officers? It won't be more than a day now before I start. We are to get the slings ready today. This clean sky and gentle swell is just the kind of thing for swinging off a dozen tons of lead and iron, isn't it?'

'It won't affect you much,' said Weybridge.

'No. Seventy or eighty feet down, and I shall be there in a dozen seconds, there's not a particle moving, though the wind shriek itself hoarse up above, and the water lifts halfway to the clouds. No. Down there—' He moved to the side of the ship and the other two followed him. All three leant forward on their elbows and stared down into the yellow-green water.

'*Peace*,' said Elstead, finishing his thought aloud.

'Are you dead certain that clockwork will act?' asked Weybridge presently.

'It has worked thirty-five times,' said Elstead. 'It's bound to work.'

'But if it doesn't?'

'Why shouldn't it?'

'I wouldn't go down in that confounded thing,' said Weybridge, 'for twenty thousand pounds.'

'Cheerful chap you are,' said Elstead, and spat sociably at a bubble below.

'I don't understand yet how you mean to work the thing,' said Steevens.

'In the first place, I'm screwed into the sphere,' said Elstead, 'and when I've turned the electric light off and on three times to show I'm cheerful, I'm slung out over the stern by that crane, with all those big lead sinkers slung below me. The top lead weight has a roller carrying a hundred fathoms of strong cord rolled up, and that's all that joins the sinkers to the sphere, except the slings that will be cut when the affair is dropped. We use cord rather than wire rope because it's easier to cut and more buoyant – necessary points, as you will see.

'Through each of these lead weights you notice there is a hole, and an iron rod will be run through that and will project six feet on the lower side. If that rod is rammed up from below, it knocks up a lever and sets the clockwork in motion at the side of the cylinder on which the cord winds.

'Very well. The whole affair is lowered gently into the water, and the slings are cut. The sphere floats – with the air in it, it's lighter than water – but the lead weights go down straight and the cord runs out. When the cord is all paid out, the sphere will go down too, pulled down by the cord.'

'But why the cord?' asked Steevens. 'Why not fasten the weights directly to the sphere?'

'Because of the smash down below. The whole affair will go rushing down, mile after mile, at a headlong pace at last. It would be knocked to pieces on the bottom if it wasn't for that cord. But the weights will hit the bottom, and directly they do the buoyancy of the sphere will come into play. It will go on sinking slower and slower; come to a stop at last, and then begin to float upward again.

'That's where the clockwork comes in. Directly the weights smash against the sea bottom, the rod will be knocked through and will kick up the clockwork, and the cord will be rewound on the reel. I shall be lugged down to the sea bottom. There I shall stay for half an hour, with the electric light on, looking about me. Then the clockwork will release a spring knife, the cord will be cut, and up I shall rush again, like a soda-water bubble. The cord itself will help the flotation.'

'And if you should chance to hit a ship?' said Weybridge.

'I should come up at such a pace, I should go clean through it,' said Elstead, 'like a cannonball. You needn't worry about that.'

'And suppose some nimble crustacean should wriggle into your clockwork—'

'It would be a pressing sort of invitation for me to stop,' said Elstead, turning his back on the water and staring at the sphere.

They had swung Elstead overboard by eleven o'clock. The day was serenely bright and calm, with the horizon lost in haze. The electric glare in the little upper compartment beamed cheerfully three times. Then they let him down slowly to the surface of the water, and a sailor in the stern chains hung ready to cut the tackle that held the lead weights and the sphere together. The globe, which had looked so large on deck, looked the smallest thing conceivable under the stern of the ship. It rolled a little, and its two dark windows, which floated uppermost, seemed like eyes turned up in round wonderment at the people who crowded the rail. A voice wondered how Elstead liked the rolling. 'Are you ready?' sang out the commander.

'Ay, Ay, sir!'

'Then let her go!'

The rope of the tackle tightened against the blade and was cut, and an eddy rolled over the globe in a grotesquely helpless fashion. Someone waved a handkerchief, someone else tried an ineffectual cheer, a middy was counting slowly, 'Eight, nine, ten!' Another roll, then with a jerk and a splash the thing righted itself.

It seemed to be stationary for a moment, to grow rapidly smaller, and then the water closed over it, and it became visible, enlarged by refraction and dimmer, below the surface. Before one could count three it had disappeared. There was a flicker of white light far down in the water, that diminished to a speck and vanished. Then there was nothing but a depth of water going down into blackness, through which a shark was swimming.

Then suddenly the screw of the cruiser began to rotate, the water was crickled, the shark disappeared in a wrinkled confusion, and a torrent of foam rushed across the crystalline clearness that had swallowed up Elstead. 'What's the idea?' said one AB to another.

'We're going to lay off about a couple of miles, 'fear he should hit us when he comes up,' said his mate.

The ship steamed slowly to her new position. Aboard her almost everyone who was unoccupied remained watching the breathing swell into which the sphere had sunk. For the next half-hour it is doubtful if a word was spoken that did not bear directly or indirectly on Elstead. The December sun was now high in the sky, and the heat very considerable.

'He'll be cold enough down there,' said Weybridge. 'They say that below a certain depth sea water's always just about freezing.'

'Where'll he come up?' asked Steevens. 'I've lost my bearings.'

'That's the spot,' said the commander, who prided himself on his omniscience. He extended a precise finger, south-eastward. 'And this, I reckon, is pretty nearly the moment,' he said. 'He's been thirty-five minutes.'

'How long does it take to reach the bottom of the ocean?' asked Steevens.

'For a depth of five miles, and reckoning – as we did – an acceleration of two feet per second, both ways, is just about threequarters of a minute.'

'Then he's overdue,' said Weybridge.

'Pretty nearly,' said the commander. 'I suppose it takes a few minutes for that cord of his to wind in.'

'I forgot that,' said Weybridge, evidently relieved.

And then began the suspense. A minute slowly dragged itself out, and no sphere shot out of the water. Another followed, and nothing broke the low oily swell. The sailors explained to one another that little point about the winding-in of the cord. The rigging was dotted with expectant faces. 'Come up, Elstead!' called one hairy-chested salt, impatiently, and the others caught it up, and shouted as though they were waiting for the curtain of a theatre to rise.

The commander glanced irritably at them.

'Of course, if the acceleration's less than two,' he said, 'he'll be all the longer. We aren't absolutely certain that was the proper figure. I'm no slavish believer in calculations.'

Steevens agreed concisely. No one on the quarter-deck spoke for a couple of minutes. Then Steevens' watchcase clicked.

When, twenty-one minutes after the sun reached the zenith, they were still waiting for the globe to reappear, not a man aboard had dared to whisper that hope was dead. It was Weybridge who first gave expression to that realisation. He spoke while the sound of eight bells still hung in the air. 'I always distrusted that window,' he said quite suddenly to Steevens.

'Good God!' said Steevens; 'you don't think—'

'Well!' said Weybridge, and left the rest to his imagination.

'I'm no great believer in calculations myself,' said the commander dubiously, 'so that I'm not altogether hopeless yet.' And at midnight the gunboat was steaming slowly in a spiral round the spot where the globe had sunk, and the white beam of the electric light fled and halted and swept discontentedly onward again over the waste of phosphorescent waters under the little stars.

'If his window hasn't burst and smashed him,' said Weybridge, 'then it's a cursed sight worse, for his clock-work has gone wrong, and he's alive now, five miles under our feet, down there in the cold and dark, anchored in that little bubble of his, where never a ray of light has shone or a human being lived, since the waters were gathered together. He's there without food, feeling hungry and thirsty and scared, wondering whether he'll starve or stifle. Which will it be? The Myers apparatus is running out, I suppose. How long do they last?'

'Good heavens!' he exclaimed, 'what little things we are! We daring little devils! Down there, miles and miles of water – all water, and all this empty water about us and this sky. Gulfs!' He threw his hands out, and as he did so, a little white streak swept noiselessly up the sky, travelled more slowly, stopped, became a motionless dot, as though a new star had fallen up into the sky. Then it went sliding back again and lost itself amidst the reflections of the stars and the white haze of the sea's phosphorescence.

At the sight he stopped, arm extended and mouth open. He shut his mouth, opened it again, and waved his arms with an impatient gesture. Then he turned, shouted 'El-stead ahoy!' to the first watch, and went at a run to Lindley and the searchlight. 'I saw him,' he said. 'Starboard there! His light's on, and he's just shot out of the water. Bring the light round. We ought to see him drifting, when he lifts on the swell.'

But they never picked up the explorer until dawn. Then they almost ran him down. The crane was swung out and a boat's crew hooked the chain to the sphere. When they had shipped the sphere, they unscrewed the manhole and peered into the darkness of the interior (for the electric light chamber was intended to illuminate the water about the sphere, and was shut off entirely from its general cavity).

The air was very hot within the cavity, and the

india-rubber at the lip of the manhole was soft. There was no answer to their eager questions and no sound of movement within. Elstead seemed to be lying motionless, crumpled up in the bottom of the globe. The ship's doctor crawled in and lifted him out to the men outside. For a moment or so they did not know whether Elstead was alive or dead. His face, in the yellow light of the ship's lamps, glistened with perspiration. They carried him down to his own cabin.

He was not dead, they found, but in a state of absolute nervous collapse, and besides cruelly bruised. For some days he had to lie perfectly still. It was a week before he could tell his experiences.

Almost his first words were that he was going down again. The sphere would have to be altered, he said, in order to allow him to throw off the cord if need be, and that was all. He had had the most marvellous experience. 'You thought I should find nothing but ooze,' he said. 'You laughed at my explorations, and I've discovered a new world!' He told his story in disconnected fragments, and chiefly from the wrong end, so that it is impossible to retell it in his words. But what follows is the narrative of his experience.

It began atrociously, he said. Before the cord ran out, the thing kept rolling over. He felt like a frog in a football. He could see nothing but the crane and the sky overhead, with an occasional glimpse of the people on the ship's rail. He couldn't tell a bit which way the thing would roll next. Suddenly he would find his feet going up, and try to step, and over he went rolling, head over heels, and just anyhow, on the padding. Any other shape would have been more comfortable, but no other shape was to be relied upon under the huge pressure of the nethermost abyss.

Suddenly the swaying ceased, the globe righted, and when he had picked himself up, he saw the water all about him greeny-blue, with an attenuated light filtering down from above, and a shoal of little floating things went rushing up past him, as it seemed to him, towards the light. And even as he looked, it grew darker and darker, until the water above was as dark as the midnight sky, albeit of a greener shade, and the water below black. And little transparent things in the water developed a faint glint of luminosity, and shot past him in greenish streaks.

And the feeling of falling! It was just like the start of a lift, he said, only it kept on. One has to imagine what that means, that keeping on. It was then of all times that Elstead repented of his adventure. He saw the chances against him in an altogether new light. He thought of the big cuttlefish people knew to exist in the middle waters, the kind of things they find half digested in whales at times, or floating dead and rotten and half eaten by fish. Suppose one caught hold and wouldn't let go. And had the clockwork really been sufficiently tested? But whether he wanted to go back mattered not the slightest now.

In fifty seconds everything was as black as night outside, except where the beam from his light struck through the waters, and picked out every now and then some fish or scrap of sinking matter. They flashed by too fast for him to see what they were. Once he thinks he passed a shark. And then the sphere began to get hot by friction against the water. They had underestimated this, it seems.

The first thing he noticed was that he was perspiring, and then he heard a hissing growing louder under his feet, and saw a lot of little bubbles – very little bubbles they were – rushing upward like a fan through the water outside. Steam! He felt the window, and it was hot. He turned on the minute glow-lamp that lit his own cavity, looked at the padded watch by the studs, and saw he had been travelling now for two minutes. It came into his head that the window would crack through the conflict of temperatures, for he knew the bottom water is very near freezing.

Then suddenly the floor of the sphere seemed to press against his feet, the rush of bubbles outside grew slower and slower, and the hissing diminished. The sphere rolled a little. The window had not cracked, nothing had given, and he knew that the dangers of sinking, at any rate, were over.

In another minute or so he would be on the floor of the abyss. He thought, he said, of Steevens and Weybridge and the rest of them five miles overhead, higher to him than the very highest clouds that ever floated over land are to us, steaming slowly and staring down and wondering what had happened to him.

He peered out of the window. There were no more bubbles now, and the hissing had stopped. Outside there was a heavy blackness – as black as black velvet – except where the electric light pierced the empty water and showed the colour of it – a yellow-green. Then three things like shapes of fire swam into sight, following each other through the water. Whether they were little and near or big and far off he could not tell.

Each was outlined in a bluish light almost as bright as the lights of a fishing smack, a light which seemed to be smoking greatly, and all along the sides of them were specks of this, like the lighter portholes of a ship. Their phosphorescence seemed to go out as they came into the radiance of his lamp, and he saw then that they were little fish of some strange sort, with huge heads, vast eyes, and dwindling bodies and tails. Their eyes were turned towards him, and he judged they were following him down. He supposed they were attracted by his glare.

Presently others of the same sort joined them. As he went on down, he noticed that the water became of a pallid colour, and that little specks twinkled in his ray like motes in a sunbeam. This was probably due to the clouds of ooze and mud that the impact of his leaden sinkers had disturbed.

By the time he was drawn down to the lead weights he was in a dense fog of white that his electric light failed altogether to pierce for more than a few yards, and many minutes elapsed before the hanging sheets of sediment subsided to any extent. Then, lit by his light and by the transient phosphorescence of a distant shoal of fishes, he was able to see under the huge blackness of the super-incumbent water an undulating expanse of greyish-white ooze, broken here and there by tangled thickets of a growth of sea lilies, waving hungry tentacles in the air.

Farther away were the graceful, translucent outlines of a group of gigantic sponges. About this floor there were scattered a number of bristling flattish tufts of rich purple and black, which he decided must be some sort of sea-urchin, and small, large-eyed or blind things having a curious resemblance, some to woodlice, and others to lobsters, crawled sluggishly across the track of the light and vanished into the obscurity again, leaving furrowed trails behind them.

Then suddenly the hovering swarm of little fishes veered about and came towards him as a flight of starlings might do. They passed over him like a phosphorescent snow, and then he saw behind them some larger creature advancing towards the sphere.

At first he could see it only dimly, a faintly moving figure remotely suggestive of a walking man, and then it came into the spray of light that the lamp shot out. As the glare struck it, it shut its eyes, dazzled. He stared in rigid astonishment.

It was a strange vertebrated animal. Its dark purple head was dimly suggestive of a chameleon, but it had such a high forehead and such a braincase as no reptile ever displayed before; the vertical pitch of its face gave it a most extraordinary resemblance to a human being.

Two large and protruding eyes projected from sockets in chameleon fashion, and it had a broad reptilian mouth with horny lips beneath its little nostrils. In the position of the ears were two huge gill-covers, and out of these floated a branching tree of coralline filaments, almost like the treelike gills that all young rays and sharks possess.

But the humanity of the face was not the most

extraordinary thing about the creature. It was a biped; its almost globular body was poised on a tripod of two frog-like legs and a long thick tail, and its fore limbs, which grotesquely caricatured the human hand, much as a frog's do, carried a long shaft of bone, tipped with copper. The colour of the creature was variegated; its head, hands, and legs were purple; but its skin, which hung loosely upon it, even as clothes might do, was a phosphorescent grey. And it stood there blinded by the light.

At last this unknown creature of the abyss blinked its eyes open, and, shading them with its disengaged hand, opened its mouth and gave vent to a shouting noise, articulate almost as speech might be, that penetrated even the steel case and padded jacket of the sphere. How a shouting may be accomplished without lungs Elstead does not profess to explain. It then moved sideways out of the glare into the mystery of shadow that bordered it on either side, and Elstead felt rather than saw that it was coming towards him. Fancying the light had attracted it, he turned the switch that cut off the current. In another moment something soft dabbed upon the steel, and the globe swayed.

Then the shouting was repeated, and it seemed to him that a distant echo answered it. The dabbing recurred, and the whole globe swayed and ground against the spindle over which the wire was rolled. He stood in the blackness and peered out into the everlasting night of the abyss. And presently he saw, very faint and remote, other phosphorescent quasi-human forms hurrying towards him.

Hardly knowing what he did, he felt about in his swaying prison for the stud of the exterior electric light, and came by accident against his own small glow-lamp in its padded recess. The sphere twisted, and then threw him down; he heard shouts like shouts of surprise, and when he rose to his feet he saw two pairs of stalked eyes peering into the lower window and reflecting his light.

In another moment hands were dabbing vigorously at his steel casing, and there was a sound, horrible enough in his position, of the metal protection of the clockwork being vigorously hammered. That, indeed, sent his heart into his mouth, for if these strange creatures succeeded in stopping that, his release would never occur. Scarcely had he thought as much when he felt the sphere sway violently, and the floor of it press hard against his feet. He turned off the small glow-lamp that lit the interior, and sent the ray of the large light in the separate compartment out into the water. The sea-floor and the man-like creatures had disappeared, and a couple of fish chasing each other dropped suddenly by the window.

He thought at once that these strange denizens of the deep sea had broken the rope, and that he had escaped. He drove up faster and faster, and then stopped with a jerk that sent him flying against the padded roof of his prison. For half a minute, perhaps, he was too astonished to think.

Then he felt that the sphere was spinning slowly, and rocking, and it seemed to him that it was also being drawn through the water. By crouching close to the window, he managed to make his weight effective and roll that part of the sphere downward, but he could see nothing save the pale ray of his light striking down ineffectively into the darkness. It occurred to him that he would see more if he turned the lamp off, and allowed his eyes to grow accustomed to the profound obscurity.

In this he was wise. After some minutes the velvety blackness became a translucent blackness, and then, far away, and as faint as the zodiacal light of an English summer evening, he saw shapes moving below. He judged these creatures had detached his cable and were towing him along the sea bottom.

And then he saw something faint and remote across the undulations of the submarine plain, a broad horizon of pale luminosity that extended this way and that way as far as the range of his little window permitted him to see. To this he was being towed, as a balloon might be towed by men out of the open country into a town. He approached it very slowly, and very slowly the dim irradiation was gathered together into more definite shapes.

It was nearly five o'clock before he came over this luminous area, and by that time he could make out an arrangement suggestive of streets and houses grouped about a vast roofless erection that was grotesquely suggestive of a ruined abbey. It was spread out like a map below him. The houses were all roofless enclosures of walls, and their substance being, as he afterwards saw, of phosphorescent bones, gave the place an appearance as if it were built of drowned moonshine.

Among the inner caves of the place waving trees of crinoid stretched their tentacles, and tall, slender, glassy sponges shot like shining minarets and lilies of filmy light out of the general glow of the city. In the open spaces of the place he could see a stirring movement as of crowds of people, but he was too many fathoms above them to distinguish the individuals in those crowds.

Then slowly they pulled him down, and as they did so, the details of the place crept slowly upon his apprehension. He saw that the courses of the cloudy buildings were marked out with beaded lines of round objects, and then he perceived that at several points below him, in broad open spaces, were forms like the encrusted shapes of ships.

Slowly and surely he was drawn down, and the forms below him became brighter, clearer, more distinct. He was being pulled down, he perceived, towards the large building in the centre of the town, and he could catch a glimpse every now and again of the multitudinous forms that were lugging at his cord. He was astonished to see that the rigging of one of the ships, which formed such a prominent feature of the place, was crowded with a host of gesticulating figures regarding him, and then the walls of the great building rose about him silently, and hid the city from his eyes.

And such walls they were, of water-logged wood, and twisted wire-rope, and iron spars, and copper, and the bones and skulls of dead men. The skulls ran in zigzag lines and spirals and fantastic curves over the buildings; and in and out of their eye-sockets, and over the whole surface of the place, lurked and played a multitude of silvery little fishes.

Suddenly his ears were filled with a low shouting and a noise like the violent blowing of horns, and this gave place to a fantastic chant. Down the sphere sank, past the huge pointed windows, through which he saw vaguely a great number of these strange ghostlike people regarding him, and at last he came to rest, as it seemed, on a kind of altar that stood in the centre of the place.

And now he was at such a level that he could see these strange people of the abyss plainly once more. To his astonishment, he perceived that they were prostrating themselves before him, all save one, dressed as it seemed in a robe of placoid scales, and crowned with a luminous diadem, who stood with his reptilian mouth opening and shutting, as though he led the chanting of the worshippers.

A curious impulse made Elstead turn on his small glow-lamp again, so that he became visible to these creatures of the abyss, albeit the glare made them disappear forthwith into night. At this sudden sight of him, the chanting gave place to a tumult of exultant shouts; and Elstead, being anxious to watch them, turned his light off again, and vanished from before their eyes. But for a time he was too blind to make out what they were doing, and when at last he could distinguish them, they were kneeling again. And thus they continued worshipping him, without rest or intermission, for a space of three hours.

Most circumstantial was Elstead's account of his astounding city and its people, these people of perpetual night, who have never seen sun or moon or stars, green vegetation, nor any living, air-breathing creatures, who know nothing of fire, nor any light but the phosphorescent light of living things.

Startling as is his story, it is yet more startling to find that scientific men, of such eminence as Adams and Jenkins, find nothing incredible in it. They tell me they see no reason why intelligent, water-breathing, vertebrated creatures inured to a low temperature and enormous pressure, and of such a heavy structure that neither alive nor dead would they float, might not live upon the bottom of the deep sea, and quite unsuspected by us, descendants like ourselves of the great Theriomorpha of the New Red Sandstone age.

We should be known to them, however, as strange, meteoric creatures, wont to fall catastrophically dead out of the mysterious blackness of their watery sky. And not only we ourselves, but our ships, our metals, our appliances, would come raining down out of the night. Sometimes sinking things would smite down and crush them, as if it were the judgement of some unseen power above, and sometimes would come things of the utmost rarity or utility, or shapes of inspiring suggestion. One can understand, perhaps, something of their behaviour at the descent of a living man, if one thinks what a barbaric people might do, to whom an enhaloed, shining creature came suddenly out of the sky.

At one time or another Elstead probably told the officers of the *Ptarmigan* every detail of his strange twelve hours in the abyss. That he also intended to write them down is certain, but he never did, and so unhappily we have to piece together the discrepant fragments of his story from the reminiscences of Commander Simmons, Weybridge, Steevens, Lindley, and the others.

We see the thing darkly in fragmentary glimpses – the huge ghostly building, the bowing, chanting people, with their dark chameleonlike heads and faintly luminous clothing, and Elstead, with his light turned on again, vainly trying to convey to their minds that the cord by which the sphere was held was to be severed. Minute after minute slipped away, and Elstead, looking at his watch, was horrified to find that he had oxygen only for four hours more. But the chant in his honour kept on as remorselessly as if it was the marching song of his approaching death.

The manner of his release he does not understand, but to judge by the end of cord that hung from the sphere, it had been cut through by rubbing against the edge of the altar. Abruptly the sphere rolled over, and he swept up, out of their world, as an ethereal creature clothed in a vacuum would sweep through our own atmosphere back to its native ether again. He must have torn out of their sight as a hydrogen bubble hastens upward from our air. A strange ascension it must have seemed to them.

The sphere rushed up with even greater velocity than, when weighted with the lead sinkers, it had rushed down. It became exceedingly hot. It drove up with the windows uppermost, and he remembers the torrent of bubbles frothing against the glass. Every moment he expected this to fly. Then suddenly something like a huge wheel seemed to be released in his head, the padded compartment began spinning about him, and he fainted. His next recollection was of his cabin, and of the doctor's voice.

But that is the substance of the extraordinary story that Elstead related in fragments to the officers of the *Ptarmigan*. He promised to write it all down at a later date. His mind was chiefly occupied with the improvement of his apparatus, which was effected at Rio.

It remains only to tell that on 2 February 1896, he made his second descent into the ocean abyss, with the improvements his first experience suggested. What happened we shall probably never know. He never returned. The *Ptarmigan* beat about over the point of his submersion, seeking him in vain for thirteen days. Then she returned to Rio, and the news was telegraphed to his friends. So the matter rests for the present. But it is hardly probable that no further attempt will be made to verify his strange story of these hitherto unsuspected cities of the deep sea.

CREATURE OF THE SNOWS

William Sambrot

Ed McKale straightened up under his load of cameras and equipment, squinting against the blasting wind, peering, staring, sweeping the jagged, unending expanse of snow and wind-scoured rock. Looking, searching, as he'd been doing now for two months, cameras at the ready.

Nothing. Nothing but the towering Himalayas, thrusting miles high on all sides, stretching in awesome grandeur from horizon to horizon, each pinnacle tipped with immense banners of snow plumes, streaming out in the wind, vivid against the darkly blue sky. The vista was one of surpassing beauty; viewing it, Ed automatically thought of light settings, focal length, colour filters – then just as automatically rejected the thought. He was here, on top of the world, to photograph something infinitely more newsworthy – if only he could find it.

The expedition paused, strung out along a ridge of blue snow, with shadows falling away to the right and left into terrifying abysses, and Ed sucked for air. Twenty thousand feet is really quite high, although many of the peaks beyond rose nearly ten thousand feet above him.

Up ahead, the Sherpa porters – each a marvellous shot, gap-toothed, ebullient grins, seamed faces, leathery brown – bowed under stupendous loads for this altitude, leaning on their coolie crutches, waiting for Doctor Schenk to make up his mind. Schenk, the expedition leader, was arguing with the guides again, his breath spurting little puffs of vapour, waving his arms, pointing – down.

Obviously Schenk was calling it quits. He was within his rights, Ed knew; two months was all Schenk had contracted for. Two months of probing snow and ice; scrambling over crevasses, up rotten rock cliffs, wind-ravaged, bleak, stretching endlessly towards Tibet and the never-never lands beyond. Two months of searching for footprints where none should be. Searching for odours, for droppings, anything to disclose the presence of creatures other than themselves. Without success.

Two months of nothing. Big, fat nothing.

The expedition was a bust. The goofiest assignment of this or any other century, as Ed felt it would be from the moment he'd sat across a desk from the big boss in the picture-magazine's New York office, two months ago, looking at the blurred photograph, while the boss filled him in on the weird details.

The photograph, his boss had told him gravely, had been taken in the Himalayan mountains, at an altitude of twenty-one thousand feet, by a man soaring overhead in a motorless glider.

'A glider,' Ed had said noncommittally, staring at the fuzzy enlarged snapshot of a great expanse of snow and rocky ledges, full of harsh light and shadows, a sort of roughly bowl-shaped plateau apparently, and in the middle of it a group of indistinct figures, tiny, lost against the immensity of great ice pinnacles. Ed looked closer. Were the figures people? If so – what had happened to their clothes?

'A glider,' his boss reiterated firmly. The glider pilot, the boss said, was manoeuvring in an undraught, attempting to do the incredible – soar over Mount Everest in a home-made glider. The wide-winged glider had been unable to achieve the flight over Everest, but, flitting silently about seeking updraughts, it cleared a jagged pinnacle and there, less than a thousand feet below, the pilot saw movement where none should have been. And dropping lower, startled, he'd seen, the boss said dryly, 'creatures – creatures that looked exactly like a group of naked men and women and kids, playing in the snow, at an altitude of twenty thousand five hundred feet.' He'd had the presence of mind to take a few hasty snapshots before the group disappeared. Only one of the pictures had developed.

Looking at the snapshot with professional scorn, Ed had said, 'These things are indistinct. I think he's selling you a bill of goods.'

'No,' the boss said, 'we checked on the guy. He really did make the glider flight. We've had experts go over that blow-up. The picture's genuine. Those are naked biped, erect-walking creatures.' He flipped the picture irritably. 'I can't publish this thing; I want close-ups, action shots, the sort of thing our subscribers have come to expect of us.'

He'd lighted a cigar slowly. 'Bring me back some pictures I can publish, Ed, and you can write your own ticket.'

'You're asking me to climb Mount Everest,' Ed said, carefully keeping the sarcasm out of his voice. 'To search for this plateau here,' he tapped the shoddy photograph, 'and take pix of – what are they, biped, erect-walking creatures, you say?'

The boss cleared his throat. 'Not Mount Everest, Ed. It's Gauri Sankar, one of the peaks near Mount Everest. Roughly, it's only about twenty-three thousand feet or so high.'

'That's pretty rough,' Ed said.

The boss looked pained. 'Actually it's not Gauri Sankar either. Just one of the lesser peaks of the Gauri Sankar massif. Well under twenty-three thousand. Certainly nothing to bother a hot-shot ex-paratrooper like you, Ed.'

Ed winced, and the boss continued, 'This guy – this glider pilot – wasn't able to pin-point the spot, but he did come up with a pretty fair map of the terrain – for a pretty fair price. We've checked it out with the American Alpine Club; it conforms well with their own charts of the general area. Several expeditions have been in the vicinity, but not this exact spot, they tell me. It's not a piece of cake by any means, but it's far from being another Annapurna, or K-Two, for accessibility.'

He sucked at his cigar thoughtfully. 'The Alpine Club says we've got only about two months of good weather before the inevitable monsoons hit that area – so time, as they say, is of the essence, Ed. But two months for this kind of thing ought to be plenty. Everything will be first class; we're even including these new gas guns that shoot hypodermic needles, or something similar. We'll fly the essentials into Katmandu and air-drop everything possible along the route up to your base at' – he squinted at a map – 'Namche Bazar. A Sherpa village which is twelve thousand feet high.'

He smiled amiably at Ed. 'That's a couple of weeks' march up from the nearest railroad, and ought to get you acclimatised nicely. Plenty of experienced porters at Namche, all Sherpas. We've lined up a couple of expert mountain climbers with Himalayan background. And the expedition leader will be Doctor Schenk – top man in his field.'

'What is his field?' Ed asked gloomily.

'Zoology. Whatever these things are in this picture, they're animal, which is his field. Everyone will be sworn to secrecy; you'll be the only one permitted to use a camera, Ed. This could be the biggest thing you'll ever cover, if these things are what I think they are.'

'What do you think they are?'

'An unknown species of man – or sub-man,' his boss said, and prudently Ed remained silent. Two months would tell the tale.

But two months didn't tell. Oh, there were plenty of wild rumours by the Nepalese all along the upper route. Hushed stories of the two-legged creatures that walked like a man. A monster the Sherpas called Yeti. Legends. Strange encounters; drums sounding from snow-swept heights; while snatches of song drifting down from peaks that were inaccessible to ordinary men. And one concrete fact: a ban laid on by the Buddhist monks, against the taking of any life in the high Himalayas. What life? Ed wondered.

Stories, legends – but nothing else.

Two months of it. Starting from the tropical flatlands, up through the lush, exotic rain forest, where sun struggled through immense trees festooned with orchids. Two months, moving up into the arid foothills, where foliage abruptly ceased and the rocks and wind took over. Up and ever up, to where the first heavy snow pack lay. And higher still, following the trail laid out by the glider pilot – and what impelled a man, Ed wondered, to soar over Mount Everest in a home-made glider?

Two months, during which Ed had come to dislike Doctor Schenk intensely. Tall, saturnine, smelling strongly of formaldehyde, Schenk classified everything into terms of vertebrate, invertebrate.

So now, standing on this wind-scoured ridge with the shadows falling into the abysses on either side, Ed peered through ice-encrusted goggles, watching Schenk arguing with the guides. He motioned to the ledge above, and obediently the Sherpas moved towards it.

Obviously that would be the final camping spot. The two months were over by several days; Schenk was within his rights to call it quits. It was only Ed's assurances that the plateau they were seeking lay just ahead that had kept Schenk from bowing out exactly on the appointed time; that and the burning desire to secure his niche in zoology forever with a new specimen: biped, erect-walking – what?

But the plateau just ahead, and the one after that, and all the rest beyond had proved just as empty as those behind.

A bust. Whatever the unknown creatures were the glider pilot had photographed, they would remain just that – unknown.

And yet, as Ed slogged slowly up towards where the porters were setting up the bright blue-and-yellow nylon tents, he was nagged by a feeling that that odd-shaped pinnacle ahead looked awfully much like the one in the blurred photograph. With his unfailing memory for pictures, Ed remembered the tall, jagged cone that had cast a black shadow across a snowy plateau, pointing directly towards the little group that was in the centre of the picture.

But Schenk wasn't having any more plateaux. He shook his head vehemently, white-daubed lips a grim line on his sun-blistered face. 'Last camp, Ed,' he said firmly. 'We agreed this would be the final plateau. I'm already a week behind schedule. If the monsoons hit us, we could be in serious trouble below. We have to get started back. I know exactly how you feel, but – I'm afraid this is it.'

Later that night, while the wind moved ceaselessly, sucking at the tent, they burrowed in sleeping bags, talking.

'There must be some basis of fact in those stories,' Ed said to Doctor Schenk. 'I've given them a lot of thought. Has it occurred to you that every one of the sightings, the few face-to-face meetings of the natives and these – these unknowns, has generally been just around dawn, and usually when the native was alone?'

Schenk smiled dubiously. 'Whatever this creature may be – and I'm convinced that it's either a species of large bear, or one of the great anthropoids – it certainly must keep off the well-travelled routes. There are very few passes through these peaks, of course, and it would be quite simple for them to avoid these locales.'

'But we're not on any known trail,' Ed said thoughtfully. 'I believe our methods have been all wrong – stringing out a bunch of men, looking for trails in the snow. All we've done is announce our presence to anything with ears for miles around. That glider pilot made no sound; he came on them without warning.'

Ed looked intently at Schenk. 'I'd like to try that peak up ahead – and the plateau beyond.' When Schenk uttered a protesting cry, Ed said, 'Wait; this time I'll go alone – with just one Sherpa guide. We could leave several hours before daybreak. No equipment, other than oxygen, food for one meal – and my cameras, of course. Maintain a strict silence. We could be back before noon. Will you wait long enough for this one last try?' Schenk hesitated. 'Only a few hours more,' Ed urged.

Schenk stared at him, then he nodded slowly. 'Agreed. But aren't you forgetting the most important item of all?' When Ed looked blank, Schenk smiled. 'The gas gun. If you should run across one, we'll need more proof than just your word for it.'

There was very little wind, no moon, but cold, the cold approaching that of outer space, as Ed and one Sherpa porter started away from the sleeping camp, up the shattered floor of an ice river that swept down from the jagged peak ahead.

They moved up, hearing only the squeak of equipment, the peculiar gritty sound of crampons biting into packed snow, an occasional hollow crash of falling ice blocks. To the east already a faint line of grey was visible; daylight was hours away, but at this tremendous height sunrise came early. They moved slowly, the thin air cutting cruelly into their lungs, moving up, up.

They stopped once for hot chocolate from a vacuum bottle, and Ed slapped the Sherpa's shoulder, grinning, pointing ahead to where the jagged peak glowed pink and gold in the first slanting rays of the sun. The Sherpa looked at the peak and quickly shifted his glance to the sky. He gave a long, careful look at the gathering clouds in the east, then muttered something, shaking his head, pointing back, back down to where the camp was hidden in the inky shadows of enormous boulders.

When Ed resumed the climb, the Sherpa removed the long nylon line which had joined them. The route was now comparatively level, on a huge sweeping expanse of snow-covered glacier that flowed about at the base of the peak. The Sherpa, no longer in the lead, began dropping behind as Ed pressed eagerly forward.

The sun was up, and with it the wind began keening again, bitterly sharp, bringing with it a scent of coming snow. In the east, beyond the jagged peak just ahead, the immense escarpment of the Himalayas was lost in approaching cloud. Ed hurried as best he could; it would snow, and soon. He'd have to make better time.

But above, the sky was blue, infinitely blue, and behind, the sun was well up, although the camp was still lost in night below. The peak thrust up ahead, near, with what appeared to be a natural pass skirting its flank. Ed made for it. As he circled an upthrust ridge of reddish, rotten rock, he glanced ahead. The plateau spread out before him, gently sloping, a natural amphitheatre full of deep, smooth snow, with peaks surrounding it, and the central peak thrusting a long black shadow directly across the centre. He paused, glancing back. The Sherpa had stopped, well below him, his face a dark blur, looking up, gesticulating frantically, pointing to the clouds. Ed motioned, then moved around leaning against the rock, peering ahead.

That great shadow against the snow was certainly

similar to the one in the photo – only, of course, the shadow pointed west now, when, later, it would point northwest, as the sun swung to the south. And when it did, most certainly it was the precise— He sucked in a sharp, lung-piercing breath.

He stared, squinting against the rising wind that seemed to blow from earth's outermost reaches. Three figures stirred slightly, and suddenly leaped into focus, almost perfectly camouflaged against the snow and wind-blasted rock. Three figures, not more than a hundred feet below him. Two small, one larger.

He leaned forward, his heart thudding terribly at this twenty-thousand-foot height. A tremor of excitement shook him. My Lord – it was true. They existed. He was looking at what was undeniably a female and two smaller – what? Apes?

They were covered with downy hair, nearly white, resembling nothing so much as tight-fitting leotards. The female was exactly like any woman on earth – except for the hair. No larger than most women, with arms slightly longer, more muscular. Thighs heavier, legs out of proportion to the trunk – shorter. Breasts full and firm. Not apes.

Hardly breathing, Ed squinted, staring, motionless. Not apes. Not standing so erectly. Not with those broad, high brows. Not with the undeniable intelligence of the two young capering about their mother. Not – and seeing this, Ed trembled against the freezing rock – not with the sudden affectionate sweep of the female as she lifted the smaller and pressed it to her breast, smoothing back hair from its face with a motion common to every human mother on earth. A wonderfully tender gesture.

What were they? Less than human? Perhaps. He couldn't be certain, but he thought he heard a faint gurgle of laughter from the female, fondling the small one, and the sound stirred him strangely. Doctor Schenk had assured him that no animal was capable of genuine laughter; only man.

But they laughed, those three, and, hearing it, watching the mother tickling the younger one, watching its delighted squirming, Ed knew that in that marvellous little grouping below, perfectly lighted, perfectly staged, he was privileged to observe one of the earth's most guarded secrets.

He should get started, shooting his pictures; afterwards he should stun the group into unconsciousness with the gas gun and then send the Sherpa back down for Doctor Schenk and the others. Clouds were massing, immensities of blue-black. Already the first few flakes of snow, huge and wet, drifted against his face.

But for a long moment more he remained motionless, oddly unwilling to do anything to destroy the harmony, the aching purity of the scene below, so vividly etched in brilliant light and shadow. The female, child slung casually on one hip, stood erect, hand shading her eyes, and Ed grinned. Artless, but perfectly posed. She was looking carefully about and above, scanning the great outcroppings of rock, obviously searching for something.

Then she paused. She was staring directly at him.

Ed froze, even though he knew he was perfectly concealed by the deep shadows of the high cliff behind him. She was still looking directly at him, and then, slowly her hand came up. She waved.

He shivered uncontrollably in the biting wind, trying to remain motionless. The two young ones suddenly began to jump up and down and show every evidence of joy. And suddenly Ed knew.

He turned slowly, very slowly, and with the sensation of a freezing knife plunging deeply into his chest, he saw the male less than five yards away.

It was huge, easily twice the size of the female below. And, crazily, Ed thought of Schenk's little lecture, given what seemed like aeons ago, in the incredible tropical grove far below, and six weeks before, where rhododendrons grew in wild profusion and enormous butterflies flitted about: 'In primitive man,' Schenk had said, 'as in the great apes today, the male was far larger than the female.'

The gas gun was hopelessly out of reach, securely strapped to his shoulder pack. Ed stared, knowing there was absolutely nothing he could do to protect himself before this creature, fully eight feet tall, with arms as big as Ed's own thighs, and eyes (*My Lord – blue eyes!*) boring into his. There was a light of savage intelligence there – and something else.

The creature made no move against him, and Ed stared at it, breathing rapidly, shallowly and with difficulty, noting with his photographer's eyes the immense chest span, the easy rise and fall of his breathing, the large, square, white teeth, the sombre cast of his face. There was long, sandy fur on the shoulders, chest and back, shortening to off-white over the rest of the magnificent torso. Ears rather small and close to the head. Short, thick neck, rising up from the broad shoulders to the back of the head in a straight line. Toes long and definitely prehensile.

They looked intently at each other across the abyss of time and mystery. Man and – what? How long, Ed wondered, had it stood there, observing him? Why hadn't it attacked? Had it been waiting for Ed to make a single threatening gesture – such as pointing a gun or camera? Seeing the calm awareness in those long, slanting, blue eyes, Ed sped a silent prayer of thanks upwards; most certainly if he had made a move for camera or gun, that move would have been his last.

They looked at each other through the falling snow, and suddenly there was a perfect instantaneous understanding between them. Ed made an awkward, half-frozen little bow, moving backwards. The great creature stood motionless, merely watching, and then Ed did a strange thing: he held out his hands, palms up, gave a wry grin – and ducked quickly around the outcropping of rock and began a plunging, sliding return down the way he'd come. In spite of the harsh, snow-laden wind, bitterly cold, he was perspiring.

Ed glanced back once. Nothing. Only the thickening veil of swift-blowing snow, blanking out the pinnacle, erasing every trace – every proof that anyone, anything, had stood there moments before. Only the snow, only the rocks, only the unending wind-filled silence of the top of the world. Nothing else.

The Sherpa was struggling up to him from below, terribly anxious to get started back; the storm was rising. Without a word they hooked up and began the groping, stumbling descent back to the last camp. They found the camp already broken, Sherpas already moving out. Schenk paused only long enough to give Ed a questioning look.

What could Ed say? Schenk was a scientist, demanding material proof: if not a corpse, at the very least a photograph. The only photographs Ed had were etched in his mind – not on film. And even if he could persuade Schenk to wait, when the storm cleared, the giant, forewarned, would be gone. Some farther peak, some remoter plateau would echo to his young ones' laughter.

Feeling not a bit bad about it, Ed gave Schenk a barely perceptible negative nod. Instantly Schenk shrugged, turned and went plunging down, into the thickening snow, back into the world of littler men. Ed trailed behind.

On the arduous trek back, through that first great storm, through the snow line, through the rain forest, hot and humid, Ed thought of the giant, back up there where the air was thin and pure.

Who, what, was he, and his race? Castaways on this planet, forever marooned, yearning for a distant, never-to-be-reached home?

Or did they date in unbroken descent from the Pleistocene – man's first beginning – when all the races of not-quite-man were giants; unable, or unwilling, to take the fork in the road that led to a smaller, cleverer man, forced to retreat higher and higher, to more remote areas, until finally there was only one corner of earth left to them – the high Himalayas?

Or were he and his kind earth's last reserves: not-yet-men, waiting for the opening of still another chapter in earth's unending mystery story?

Whatever the giant was, his secret was safe with him, Ed thought. For who would believe it – even if he chose to tell?

CRY OF THE HUNTERS

William Golding

In a nuclear World War an aircraft carrying evacuee schoolboys crashes on an uninhabited Pacific island. The only survivors are schoolboys, but far from behaving like responsible adults in the manner of boys portrayed in stories like *Coral Island*, they fail to organise their lives and rapidly sink to the condition of painted and superstitious savages, living in fear of a supposed Beast. The conch shell, a symbol of law and order, which was used to gather the boys for discussion of their problems, has been shattered. Piggy, a brainy boy who stubbornly defended the values of the adult world, has been killed, and Simon, the only boy brave enough to discover what the Beast really is, has been slaughtered like a pig. In the concluding chapter Ralph, an unimaginative but basically decent boy, who was originally voted leader, is hunted down by the rest of the boys, who are under the control of Jack, formerly Head Choirboy, but now a kind of tribal chief, out for blood – and not for the first time!

Ralph lay in a covert, wondering about his wounds. The bruised flesh was inches in diameter over his right ribs, with a swollen and bloody scar where the spear had hit him. His hair was full of dirt and tapped like the tendrils of a creeper. All over he was scratched and bruised from his flight through the forest. By the time his breathing was normal again, he had worked out that bathing these injuries would have to wait. How could you listen for naked feet if you were splashing in water? How could you be safe by the little stream or on the open beach?

Ralph listened. He was not really far from the Castle Rock, and during the first panic he had thought he heard sounds of pursuit. But the hunters had only sneaked into the fringes of the greenery, retrieving spears perhaps, and then had rushed back to the sunny rock as if terrified of the darkness under the leaves. He had even glimpsed one of them, striped brown, black, and red, and had judged that it was Bill. But really, thought Ralph, this was not Bill. This was a savage whose image refused to blend with that ancient picture of a boy in shorts and shirt.

The afternoon died away; the circular spots of sunlight moved steadily over green fronds and brown fibre but no sound came from behind the Rock. At last Ralph wormed out of the ferns and sneaked forward to the edge of that impenetrable thicket that fronted the neck of land. He peered with elaborate caution between branches at the edge and could see Robert sitting on guard at the top of the cliff. He held a spear in his left hand and was tossing up a pebble and catching it again with the right. Behind him a column of smoke rose thickly, so that Ralph's nostrils flared and his mouth dribbled. He wiped his nose and mouth with the back of his hand and for the first time since the morning felt hungry. The tribe must be sitting round the gutted pig, watching the fat ooze and burn among the ashes. They would be intent.

Another figure, an unrecognisable one, appeared by Robert and gave him something, then turned and went back behind the rock. Robert laid his spear on the rock beside him and began to gnaw between his raised hands. So the feast was beginning and the watchman had been given his portion.

Ralph saw that for the time being he was safe. He limped away through the fruit trees, drawn by the thought of the poor food yet bitter when he remembered the feast. Feast today, and then tomorrow. . . .

He argued unconvincingly that they would let him alone; perhaps even make an outlaw of him. But then the fatal unreasoning knowledge came to him again. The breaking of the conch and the deaths of Piggy and Simon lay over the island like a vapour. These painted savages would go further and further. Then there was that indefinable connection between himself and Jack; who therefore would never let him alone; never.

He paused, sun-flecked, holding up a bough, prepared to duck under it. A spasm of terror set him shaking and he cried aloud.

'No. They're not as bad as that. It was an accident.'

He ducked under the bough, ran clumsily, then stopped and listened.

He came to the smashed acres of fruit and ate greedily. He saw two littluns and, not having any idea of his own appearance, wondered why they screamed and ran.

When he had eaten he went towards the beach. The sunlight was slanting now into the palms by the wrecked shelter. There was the platform and the pool. The best thing to do was to ignore this leaden feeling about the heart and rely on their common sense, their daylight sanity. Now that the tribe had eaten, the thing to do was to try again. And anyway, he couldn't stay here all night in an empty shelter by the deserted platform. His flesh crept and he shivered in the evening sun. No fire; no smoke; no rescue. He turned and limped away through the forest towards Jack's end of the island.

The slanting sticks of sunlight were lost among the branches. At length he came to a clearing in the forest where rock prevented vegetation from growing. Now it was a pool of shadows and Ralph nearly flung himself behind a tree when he saw something standing in the centre; but then he saw that the white face was bone and that the pig's skull grinned at him from the top of a stick. He walked slowly into the middle of the clearing and looked steadily at the skull that gleamed as white as ever the conch had done and seemed to jeer at him cynically. An inquisitive ant was busy in one of the eye sockets but otherwise the thing was lifeless.

Or was it?

Little prickles of sensation ran up and down his back. He stood, the skull about on a level with his face, and held up his hair with two hands. The teeth grinned, the empty sockets seemed to hold his gaze masterfully and without effort.

What was it?

The skull regarded Ralph like one who knows all the answers and won't tell. A sick fear and rage swept him. Fiercely he hit out at the filthy thing in front of him that bobbed like a toy and came back, still grinning into his face, so that he lashed and cried out in loathing. Then he was licking his bruised knuckles and looking at the bare stick, while the skull lay in two pieces, its grin now six feet across. He wrenched the quivering stick from the crack and held it as a spear between him and the white pieces. Then he backed away, keeping his face to the skull that lay grinning at the sky.

When the green glow had gone from the horizon and night was fully accomplished, Ralph came again to the thicket in front of the Castle Rock. Peeping through, he could see that the height was still occupied, and whoever it was up there had a spear at the ready.

He knelt among the shadows and felt his isolation bitterly. They were savages it was true; but they were human, and the ambushing fears of the deep night were coming on.

Ralph moaned faintly. Tired though he was, he could not relax and fall into a well of sleep for fear of the tribe. Might it not be possible to walk boldly into the fort, say – 'I've got pax,' laugh lightly and sleep among the others? Pretend they were still boys, schoolboys who had said 'Sir, yes, Sir' – and worn caps? Daylight might have answered yes; but darkness and the horrors of death said no. Lying there in the darkness, he knew he was an outcast.

''Cos I had some sense.'

He rubbed his cheek along his forearm, smelling the acrid scent of salt and sweat and the staleness of dirt. Over to the left, the waves of ocean were breathing, sucking down, then boiling back over the rock.

There were sounds coming from behind the Castle Rock. Listening carefully, detaching his mind from the swing of the sea, Ralph could make out a familiar rhythm.

'*Kill the beast! Cut his throat! Spill his blood!*'

The tribe was dancing. Somewhere on the other side of this rocky wall there would be a dark circle, a glowing fire, and meat. They would be savouring food and the comfort of safety.

A noise nearer at hand made him quiver. Savages were clambering up the Castle Rock, right up to the top, and he could hear voices. He sneaked forward a few yards and saw the shape at the top of the rock change and enlarge. There were only two boys on the island who moved or talked like that.

Ralph put his head down on his forearms and accepted this new fact like a wound. Samneric were part of the tribe now. They were guarding the Castle Rock against him. There was no chance of rescuing them and building up an outlaw tribe at the other end of the island. Samneric were savages like the rest; Piggy was dead, and the conch smashed to powder.

At length the guard climbed down. The two that

remained seemed nothing more than a dark extension of the rock. A star appeared behind them and was momentarily eclipsed by some movement.

Ralph edged forward, feeling his way over the uneven surface as though he were blind. There were miles of vague water at his right and the restless ocean lay under his left hand, as awful as the shaft of a pit. Every minute the water breathed round the death rock and flowered into a field of whiteness. Ralph crawled until he found the ledge of the entry in his grasp. The lookouts were immediately above him and he could see the end of a spear projecting over the rock.

He called very gently.

'Samneric—'

There was no reply. To carry he must speak louder; and this would rouse those striped and inimical creatures from their feasting by the fire. He set his teeth and started to climb, finding the holds by touch. The stick that had supported a skull hampered him but he would not be parted from his only weapon. He was nearly level with the twins before he spoke again.

'Samneric—'

He heard a cry and a flurry from the rock. The twins had grabbed each other and were gibbering.

'It's me. Ralph.'

Terrified that they would run and give the alarm, he hauled himself up until his head and shoulders stuck over the top. Far below his armpit he saw the luminous flowering round the rock.

'It's only me. Ralph.'

At length they bent forward and peered in his face.

'We thought it was—'

' – we didn't know what it was—'

' – we thought—'

Memory of their new and shameful loyalty came to them. Eric was silent but Sam tried to do his duty.

'You got to go, Ralph. You go away now —'

He wagged his spear and essayed fierceness.

'You shove off. See?'

Eric nodded agreement and jabbed his spear in the air. Ralph leaned on his arms and did not go.

'I came to see you two.'

His voice was thick. His throat was hurting him now though it had received no wound.

'I came to see you two—'

Words could not express the dull pain of these things. He fell silent, while the vivid stars were spilt and danced all ways.

Sam shifted uneasily.

'Honest, Ralph, you'd better go.'

Ralph looked up again.

'You two aren't painted. How can you—? If it were light—'

If it were light shame would burn them at admitting these things. But the night was dark. Eric took up; and then the twins started their antiphonal speech.

'You got to go because it's not safe—'

' – they made us. They hurt us—'

'Who? Jack?'

'Oh no—'

They bent to him and lowered their voices.

'Push off, Ralph—'

' – it's a tribe—'

' – they made us—'

' – we couldn't help it—'

When Ralph spoke again his voice was low, and seemed breathless.

'What have I done? I liked him – and I wanted us to be rescued—'

Again the stars spilled about the sky. Eric shook his head, earnestly.

'Listen, Ralph. Never mind what's sense. That's gone—'

'Never mind about the chief—'

' – you got to go for your own good.'

'The chief and Roger—'

' – yes, Roger—'

'They hate you, Ralph. They're going to do you.'

'They're going to hunt you tomorrow.'

'But why?'

'I dunno. And Ralph, Jack, the Chief, says it'll be dangerous—'

' – and we've got to be careful and throw our spears like at a pig.'

'We're going to spread out in a line across the island—'

' – we're going forward from this end—'

' – until we find you.'

'We've got to give signals like this.'

Eric raised his head and achieved a faint ululation by beating on his open mouth. Then he glanced behind him nervously.

'Like that—'

' – only louder, of course.'

'But I've done nothing,' whispered Ralph, urgently. 'I only wanted to keep up a fire!'

He paused for a moment, thinking miserably of the morrow. A matter of overwhelming importance occurred to him.

'What are you—?'

He could not bring himself to be specific at first; but then fear and loneliness goaded him.

'When they find me, what are they going to do?'

The twins were silent. Beneath him, the death rock flowered again.

'What are they – oh God! I'm hungry—'

The towering rock seemed to sway under him.

'Well – what—?'

The twins answered his question indirectly.

'You got to go now, Ralph.'

'For your own good.'

'Keep away. As far as you can.'

'Won't you come with me? Three of us – we'd stand a chance.'

After a moment's silence, Sam spoke in a strangled voice.

'You don't know Roger. He's a terror.'

'– And the Chief – they're both—'

'– terrors—'

'– only Roger—'

Both boys froze. Someone was climbing towards them from the tribe.

'He's coming to see if we're keeping watch. Quick, Ralph!'

As he prepared to let himself down the cliff, Ralph snatched at the last possible advantage to be wrung out of this meeting.

'I'll lie up close; in that thicket down there,' he whispered, 'so keep them away from it. They'll never think to look so close—'

The footsteps were still some distance away.

'Sam – I'm going to be all right, aren't I?'

The twins were silent again.

'Here!' said Sam suddenly. 'Take this—'

Ralph felt a chunk of meat pushed against him and grabbed it.

'But what are you going to do when you catch me?'

Silence above. He sounded silly to himself. He lowered himself down the rock.

'What are you going to do—?'

From the top of the towering rock came the incomprehensible reply.

'Roger sharpened a stick at both ends.'

Roger sharpened a stick at both ends. Ralph tried to attach a meaning to this but could not. He used all the bad words he could think of in a fit of temper that passed into yawning. How long could you go without sleep? He yearned for a bed and sheets – but the only whiteness here was the slow spilt milk, luminous round the rock forty feet below, where Piggy had fallen. Piggy was everywhere, was on this neck, was become terrible in darkness and death. If Piggy were to come back now out of the water, with his empty head – Ralph whimpered and yawned like a littlun. The stick in his hand became a crutch on which he reeled.

Then he tensed again. There were voices raised on the

top of the Castle Rock. Samneric were arguing with someone. But the ferns and the grass were near. That was the place to be in, hidden, and next to the thicket that would serve for tomorrow's hide-out. Here – and his hands touched grass – was a place to be in for the night, not far from the tribe, so that if the horrors of the supernatural emerged one could at least mix with humans for the time being, even if it meant. . . .

What did it mean? A stick sharpened at both ends. What was there in that? They had thrown spears and missed; all but one. Perhaps they would miss next time, too.

He squatted down in the tall grass, remembered the meat that Sam had given him, and began to tear at it ravenously. While he was eating, he heard fresh noises – cries of pain from Samneric, cries of panic, angry voices. What did it mean? Someone besides himself was in trouble for at least one of the twins was catching it. Then the voices passed away down the rock and he ceased to think of them. He felt with his hands and found cool, delicate fronds backed against the thicket. Here then was the night's lair. At first light he would creep into the thicket, squeeze between the twisted stems, ensconce himself so deep that only a crawler like himself could come through; and that crawler would be jabbed. There he would sit, and the search would pass him by, and the cordon waver on, ululating along the island, and he would be free.

He pulled himself between the ferns, tunnelling in. He laid the stick beside him, and huddled himself down in the blackness. One must remember to wake at first light, in order to diddle the savages – and he did not know how quickly sleep came and hurled him down a dark interior slope.

He was awake before his eyes were open, listening to a noise that was near. He opened an eye, found the mould an inch or so from his face and his fingers gripped into it, light filtering between the fronds of fern. He had just time to realise that the age-long nightmares of falling and death were past and that the morning was come, when he heard the sound again. It was an ululation over by the seashore – and now the next savage answered and the next. The cry swept by him across the narrow end of the island from sea to lagoon, like the cry of a flying bird. He took no time to consider but grabbed his sharp stick and wriggled back among the ferns. Within seconds he was worming his way into the thicket; but not before he had glimpsed the legs of a savage coming towards him. The ferns were thumped and beaten and he heard legs moving in the long grass. The savage, whoever he was, ululated twice; and the cry was repeated in both directions, then died away. Ralph crouched still, tangled in the mid-brake, and for a time he heard nothing.

At last he examined the brake itself. Certainly no one could attack him here – and moreover he had a stroke of luck. The great rock that had killed Piggy had bounded into this thicket and bounced there, right in the centre, making a smashed space a few feet in extent each way. When Ralph had wriggled into this he felt secure, and clever. He sat down carefully among the smashed stems and waited for the hunt to pass. Looking up between the leaves he caught a glimpse of something red. That must be the top of the Castle Rock, distant and unmenacing. He composed himself triumphantly, to hear the sounds of the hunt dying away.

Yet no one made a sound; and as the minutes passed, in the green shade, his feeling of triumph faded.

At last he heard a voice – Jack's voice, but hushed.

'Are you certain?'

The savage addressed said nothing. Perhaps he made a gesture.

Roger spoke.

'If you're fooling us—'

Immediately after this, there came a gasp, and a squeal of pain. Ralph crouched instinctively. One of the twins was there, outside the thicket, with Jack and Roger.

'You're sure he meant in there?'

The twin moaned faintly and then squealed again.

'He meant he'd hide in there?'

'Yes – yes – oh—!'

Silvery laughter scattered among the trees.

So they knew.

Ralph picked up his stick and prepared for battle. But what could they do? It would take them a week to break a path through the thicket; and anyone who wormed his way in would be helpless. He felt the point of his spear with his thumb and grinned without amusement. Whoever tried that would be stuck, squealing like a pig.

They were going away, back to the tower rock. He could hear feet moving and then someone sniggered. There came again that high, bird-like cry that swept along the line. So some were still watching for him; but some—?

There was a long, breathless silence. Ralph found that he had bark in his mouth from the gnawed spear. He stood and peered upwards to the Castle Rock.

As he did so, he heard Jack's voice from the top.

'Heave! Heave! Heave!'

The red rock that he could see at the top of the cliff vanished like a curtain, and he could see figures and blue sky. A moment later the earth jolted, there was a rushing sound in the air, and the top of the thicket was cuffed as with a gigantic hand. The rock bounded on, thumping and smashing towards the beach, while a shower of broken twigs and leaves fell on him. Beyond the thicket, the tribe was cheering.

Silence again.

Ralph put his fingers in his mouth and bit them. There was only one other rock up there that they might conceivably move; but that was half as big as a cottage, big as a car, a tank. He visualised its probable progress with agonising clearness – that one would start slowly, drop from ledge to ledge, trundle across the neck like an outsize steam-roller.

'Heave! Heave! Heave!'

Ralph put down his spear, then picked it up again. He pushed his hair back irritably, took two hasty steps across the little space and then came back. He stood looking at the broken ends of branches.

Still silence.

He caught sight of the rise and fall of his diaphragm and was surprised to see how quickly he was breathing. Just left of centre, his heartbeats were visible. He put the spear down again.

'Heave! Heave! Heave!'

A shrill, prolonged cheer.

Something boomed up on the red rock, then the earth jumped and began to shake steadily, while the noise as steadily increased. Ralph was shot into the air, thrown down, dashed against branches. At his right hand, and only a few feet away, the whole thicket bent and the roots screamed as they came out of the earth together. He saw something red that turned over slowly as a mill-wheel. Then the red thing was past and the elephantine progress diminished towards the sea.

Ralph knelt on the ploughed-up soil, and waited for the earth to come back. Presently the white, broken stumps, the split sticks and the tangle of the thicket refocused. There was a kind of heavy feeling in his body where he had watched his own pulse.

Silence again.

Yet not entirely so. They were whispering out there; and suddenly the branches were shaken furiously at two places on his right. The pointed end of a stick appeared. In panic, Ralph thrust his own stick through the crack and struck with all his might.

'Aaa-ah!'

His spear twisted a little in his hands and then he withdrew it again.

'Ooh-ooh—'

Someone was moaning outside and a babble of voices rose. A fierce argument was going on and the wounded savage kept groaning. Then when there was silence, a single voice spoke and Ralph decided that it was not Jack's.

'See? I told you – he's dangerous.'

The wounded savage moaned again.

What else? What next?

Ralph fastened his hands round the chewed spear and his hair fell. Someone was muttering, only a few yards away towards the Castle Rock. He heard a savage say 'No!' in a shocked voice; and then there was suppressed laughter. He squatted back on his heels and showed his teeth at the wall of branches. He raised his spear, snarled a little, and waited.

Once more the invisible group sniggered. He heard a curious trickling sound and then a louder crepitation as if someone were unwrapping great sheets of cellophane. A stick snapped and he stifled a cough. Smoke was seeping through the branches in white and yellow wisps, the patch of blue sky overhead turned to the colour of a storm cloud, and then the smoke billowed round him.

Someone laughed excitedly, and a voice shouted.

'Smoke!'

He wormed his way through the thicket towards the forest, keeping as far as possible beneath the smoke. Presently he saw open space, and the green leaves of the edge of the thicket. A smallish savage was standing between him and the rest of the forest, a savage striped red and white, and carrying a spear. He was coughing and smearing the paint about his eyes with the back of his hand as he tried to see through the increasing smoke. Ralph launched himself like a cat; stabbed, snarling, with the spear, and the savage doubled up. There was a shout from beyond the thicket and then Ralph was running with the swiftness of fear through the undergrowth. He came to a pig-run, followed it for perhaps a hundred yards, and then swerved off. Behind him the ululation swept across the island once more and a single voice shouted three times. He guessed that was the signal to advance and sped away again, till his chest was like fire. Then he flung himself down under a bush and waited for a moment till his breathing steadied. He passed his tongue tentatively over his teeth and lips and heard far off the ululation of the pursuers.

There were many things he could do. He could climb a tree – but that was putting all his eggs in one basket. If he were detected, they had nothing more difficult to do than wait.

If only one had time to think!

Another double cry at the same distance gave him a clue to their plan. Any savage baulked in the forest would utter the double shout and hold up the line till he was free again. That way they might hope to keep the cordon unbroken right across the island. Ralph thought of the boar that had broken through them with such ease. If necessary, when the chase came too close, he could charge the cordon while it was still thin, burst through, and run back. But run back where? The cordon would turn and sweep again. Sooner or later he would have to sleep or eat – and then he would awaken with hands clawing at him; and the hunt would become a running down.

What was to be done, then? The tree? Burst the line like a boar? Either way the choice was terrible.

A single cry quickened his heart-beat and, leaping up, he dashed away towards the ocean side and the thick jungle till he was hung up among creepers; he stayed there for a moment with his calves quivering. If only one could have pax, a long pause, a time to think!

And there again, shrill and inevitable, was the ululation sweeping across the island. At that sound he shied like a horse among the creepers and ran once more till he was panting. He flung himself down by some ferns. The tree, or the charge? He mastered his breathing for a moment, wiped his mouth, and told himself to be calm. Samneric were somewhere in that line, and hating it. Or were they? And supposing, instead of them, he met the chief, or Roger who carried death in his hands?

Ralph pushed back his tangled hair and wiped the sweat out of his best eye. He spoke aloud.

'Think.'

What was the sensible thing to do?

There was no Piggy to talk sense. There was no solemn assembly for debate nor dignity of the conch.

'Think.'

Most, he was beginning to dread the curtain that might waver in his brain, blacking out the sense of danger, making a simpleton of him.

A third idea would be to hide so well that the advancing line would pass without discovering him.

He jerked his head off the ground and listened. There was another noise to attend to now – a deep grumbling noise, as though the forest itself were angry with him, a sombre noise across which the ululations were scribbled excruciatingly as on slate. He knew he had heard it before somewhere, but had no time to remember.

Break the line.

A tree.

Hide, and let them pass.

A nearer cry stood him on his feet and immediately he was away again, running fast among thorns and brambles. Suddenly he blundered into the open, found himself again in that open space – and there was the fathom-wide grin of the skull, no longer ridiculing a deep blue patch of sky but jeering up into a blanket of smoke. Then Ralph was running beneath trees, with the grumble of the forest explained. They had smoked him out and set the island on fire.

Hide was better than a tree because you had a chance of breaking the line if you were discovered.

Hide, then.

He wondered if a pig would agree, and grimaced at nothing. Find the deepest thicket, the darkest hole on the island, and creep in. Now, as he ran, he peered about him. Bars and splashes of sunlight flitted over him and sweat made glistening streaks on his dirty body. The cries were far now, and faint.

At last he found what seemed to him the right place, though the decision was desperate. Here, bushes and a wild tangle of creeper made a mat that kept out all the light of the sun. Beneath it was a space, perhaps a foot high, though it was pierced everywhere by parallel and rising stems. If you wormed into the middle of that you would be five yards from the edge, and hidden, unless the savage chose to lie down and look for you; and even then, you would be in darkness – and if the worst happened and he saw you, then you had a chance to burst out at him, fling the whole line out of step and double back.

Cautiously, his stick trailing behind him, Ralph wormed between the rising stems. When he reached the middle of the mat he lay and listened.

The fire was a big one and the drum-roll that he had thought was left so far behind was nearer. Couldn't a fire out-run a galloping horse? He could see the sun-splashed ground over an area of perhaps fifty yards from where he lay: and as he watched, the sunlight in every patch blinked at him. This was so like the curtain that flapped in his brain that for a moment he thought the blinking was inside him. But then the patches blinked more rapidly, dulled and went out, so that he saw that a great heaviness of smoke lay between the island and the sun.

If anyone peered under the bushes and chanced to glimpse human flesh it might be Samneric who would pretend not to see and say nothing. He laid his cheek against the chocolate-coloured earth, licked his dry lips and closed his eyes. Under the thicket, the earth was vibrating very slightly; or perhaps there was a sound beneath the obvious thunder of the fire and scribbled ululations that was too low to hear.

Someone cried out. Ralph jerked his cheek off the earth and looked into the dulled light. They must be near now, he thought, and his chest began to thump. Hide, break the line, climb a tree – which was the best after all? The trouble was you only had one chance.

Now the fire was nearer; those volleying shots were great limbs, trunks even, bursting. The fools! The fools!

The fire must be almost at the fruit trees – what would they eat tomorrow?

Ralph stirred restlessly in his narrow bed. One chanced nothing! What could they do? Beat him? So what? Kill him? A stick sharpened at both ends.

The cries, suddenly nearer, jerked him up. He could see a striped savage moving hastily out of a green tangle, and coming towards the mat where he hid, a savage who carried a spear. Ralph gripped his fingers into the earth. Be ready now, in case.

Ralph fumbled to hold his spear so that it was point foremost; and now he saw that the stick was sharpened at both ends.

The savage stopped fifteen yards away and uttered his cry.

Perhaps he can hear my heart over the noises of the fire. Don't scream. Get ready.

The savage moved forward so that you could only see him from the waist down. That was the butt of his spear. Now you could see him from the knee down. Don't scream.

A herd of pigs came squealing out of the greenery behind the savage and rushed away into the forest. Birds were screaming, mice shrieking, and a little hopping thing came under the mat and cowered.

Five yards away the savage stopped, standing right by the thicket, and cried out. Ralph drew his feet up and crouched. The stake was in his hands, the stake sharpened at both ends, the stake that vibrated so wildly, that grew long, short, light, heavy, light again.

The ululation spread from shore to shore. The savage knelt down by the edge of the thicket, and there were lights flickering in the forest behind him. You could see a knee disturb the mould. Now the other. Two hands. A spear.

A face.

The savage peered into the obscurity beneath the thicket. You could tell that he saw light on this side and on that, but not in the middle – there. In the middle was a blob of dark and the savage wrinkled up his face, trying to decipher the darkness.

The seconds lengthened. Ralph was looking straight into the savage's eyes.

Don't scream.

You'll get back.

Now he's seen you. He's making sure. A stick sharpened.

Ralph screamed, a scream of fright and anger and desperation. His legs straightened, the screams became continuous and foaming. He shot forward, burst the thicket, was in the open, screaming, snarling, bloody. He swung the stake and the savage tumbled over; but there were others coming towards him, crying out. He swerved as a spear flew past and then was silent, running. All at once the lights flickering ahead of him merged together, the roar of the forest rose to thunder and a tall bush directly in his path burst into a great fan-shaped flame. He swung to the right, running desperately fast, with the heat beating on his left side and the fire racing forward like a tide. The ululation rose behind him and spread along, a series of short sharp cries, the sighting call. A brown figure showed up at his right and fell away. They were all running, all crying out madly. He could hear them crashing in the undergrowth and on the left was the hot, bright thunder of the fire. He forgot his wounds, his hunger and thirst, and became fear; hopeless fear on flying feet, rushing through the forest towards the open beach. Spots jumped before his eyes and turned into red circles that expanded quickly till they passed out of sight. Below him, someone's legs were getting tired and the desperate ululation advanced like a jagged fringe of menace and was almost overhead.

He stumbled over a root and the cry that pursued him rose even higher. He saw a shelter burst into flames and the fire flapped at his right shoulder and there was the glitter of water. Then he was down, rolling over and over in the warm sand, crouching with arm up to ward off, trying to cry for mercy.

He staggered to his feet, tensed for more terrors, and looked up at a huge peaked cap. It was a white-topped cap, and above the green shade of the peak was a crown, an anchor, gold foliage. He saw white drill, epaulettes, a revolver, a row of gilt buttons down the front of a uniform.

A naval officer stood on the sand, looking down at Ralph in wary astonishment. On the beach behind him was a cutter, her bows hauled up and held by two ratings. In the stern-sheets another rating held a sub-machine gun.

The ululation faltered and died away.

The officer looked at Ralph doubtfully for a moment, then took his hand away from the butt of the revolver.

'Hullo.'

Squirming a little, conscious of his filthy appearance, Ralph answered shyly.

'Hullo.'

The officer nodded, as if a question had been answered.

'Are there any adults – any grown-ups with you?'

Dumbly, Ralph shook his head. He turned a half-pace on the sand. A semicircle of little boys, their bodies streaked with coloured clay, sharp sticks in their hands, were standing on the beach making no noise at all.

'Fun and games,' said the officer.

The fire reached the coconut palms by the beach and swallowed them noisily. A flame, seemingly detached, swung like an acrobat and licked up the palm heads on the platform. The sky was black.

The officer grinned cheerfully at Ralph.

'We saw your smoke. What have you been doing? Having a war or something?'

Ralph nodded.

The officer inspected the little scarecrow in front of

him. The kid needed a bath, a hair-cut, a nose-wipe and a good deal of ointment.

'Nobody killed, I hope? Any dead bodies?'

'Only two. And they've gone.'

The officer leaned down and looked closely at Ralph.

'Two? Killed?'

Ralph nodded again. Behind him, the whole island was shuddering with flame. The officer knew, as a rule, when people were telling the truth. He whistled softly.

Other boys were appearing now, tiny tots some of them, brown, with the distended bellies of small savages. One of them came close to the officer and looked up.

'I'm, I'm—'

But there was no more to come. Percival Wemys Madison sought in his head for an incantation that had faded clean away.

The officer turned back to Ralph.

'We'll take you off. How many of you are there?'

Ralph shook his head. The officer looked past him to the group of painted boys.

'Who's boss here?'

'I am,' said Ralph loudly.

A little boy who wore the remains of an extraordinary black cap on his red hair and who carried the remains of a pair of spectacles at his waist, started forward, then changed his mind and stood still.

'We saw your smoke. And you don't know how many of you there are?'

'No, sir.'

'I should have thought,' said the officer as he visualised the search before him. 'I should have thought that a pack of British boys – you're all British, aren't you? – would have been able to put up a better show than that – I mean—'

'It was like that at first,' said Ralph, 'before things—'

He stopped.

'We were together then—'

The officer nodded helpfully.

'I know. Jolly good show. Like the Coral Island.'

Ralph looked at him dumbly. For a moment he had a fleeting picture of the strange glamour that had once invested the beaches. But the island was scorched up like dead wood – Simon was dead – and Jack had. . . . The tears began to flow and sobs shook him. He gave himself up to them now for the first time on the island; great, shuddering spasms of grief that seemed to wrench his whole body. His voice rose under the black smoke before the burning wreckage of the island; and infected by that emotion, the other little boys began to shake and sob too. And in the middle of them, with filthy body, matted hair, and unwiped nose, Ralph wept for the end of innocence, the darkness of man's heart, and the fall through the air of the true, wise friend called Piggy.

The officer, surrounded by these noises, was moved and a little embarrassed. He turned away to give them time to pull themselves together; and waited, allowing his eyes to rest on the trim cruiser in the distance.

More Beaver Books

We hope you have enjoyed this Beaver Book. Here are some of the other titles:

The Beaver Book of Spy Stories A Beaver original. Fifteen exciting true stories of international espionage from the 1930s to the 1960s, including the Lonsdale/Kroger spy ring, Russia's master spy Rudolf Abel and the U2 incident. Compiled by George Kay and illustrated by Peter Dennis

Falcon Island A Beaver original. Set in Western Australia, this is an exciting adventure story in which Jock, Paul and Kate try to find a sunken treasure ship and save their beautiful island from mining speculators. Written by Joan Ambrose, it is the book on which the TV series *Falcon Island* is based

The Beaver Book of Animal Verse A Beaver original. A beautiful collection of poetry about all kinds of animals, compiled by Raymond Wilson, with superb line drawings by Tessa Barwick

These and many other Beavers are available from your local bookshop or newsagent, or can be ordered direct from: Hamlyn Paperback Cash Sales, PO Box 11, Falmouth, Cornwall TR10 9EN. Send a cheque or postal order made payable to the Hamlyn Publishing Group, for the price of the book plus postage at the following rates:
UK: 45p for the first book, 20p for the second book, and 14p for each additional book ordered to a maximum charge of £1.63;
BFPO and Eire: 45p for the first book, 20p for the second book, plus 14p per copy for the next 7 books and thereafter 8p per book;
OVERSEAS: 75p for the first book and 21p for each extra book.

New Beavers are published every month and if you would like the *Beaver Bulletin*, a newsletter which tells you about new books and gives a complete list of titles and prices, send a large stamped addressed envelope to:

Beaver Bulletin
The Hamlyn Group
Astronaut House
Feltham
Middlesex TW14 9AR

204790